BS

Let Us Attend

Lent 2008

Ramon ~
Lenten Blessings !

Bill

Lent 2008

Janet —

Lenten Blessing!

Phil

Let Us Attend

✦

Reflections on the Gospel of Mark for the Lenten Season

William C. Mills

iUniverse, Inc.
New York Lincoln Shanghai

Let Us Attend
Reflections on the Gospel of Mark for the Lenten Season

iUniverse books may be ordered through booksellers or by contacting:

iUniverse
2021 Pine Lake Road, Suite 100
Lincoln, NE 68512
www.iuniverse.com
1-800-Authors (1-800-288-4677)

Because of the dynamic nature of the Internet, any Web addresses or links contained in this book may have changed since publication and may no longer be valid.

The views expressed in this work are solely those of the author and do not necessarily reflect the views of the publisher, and the publisher hereby disclaims any responsibility for them.

ISBN: 978-0-595-48044-9 (pbk)
ISBN: 978-0-595-60143-1 (ebk)

Printed in the United States of America

Father Stephen J. Hrycyniak

Friend and Mentor

*"This life has been given to you for repentance.
Do not waste it in vain pursuits."*

—St. Isaac of Syria

Contents

Prayer Before the Gospel

✦

(From the Divine Liturgy of Saint John Chrysostom)

Illumine our hearts O master who loves mankind, with the pure light of Thy divine knowledge. Open the eyes of our mind to the understanding of Thy gospel teachings. Implant also in us the fear of Thy blessed commandments, that, trampling down all carnal desires, we may enter upon a spiritual manner of living, both thinking and doing such things as are well pleasing unto Thee. For Thou art the illumination of our souls and bodies, O Christ our God, and unto Thee we ascribe glory, together with Thy Father, who is from everlasting, and Thine all-holy, good, and life-creating Spirit, now and ever and unto ages of ages. Amen.

Introduction

In the springtime we enter into the liturgical season called Great Lent, which is sometimes referred to, as the Lenten Spring.[1] During Lent we return back to the basics expressed in the Scriptures, namely being more open to loving God through serving our neighbor. Jesus reminds us that all of the Old Testament Law and the Prophets can be reduced to the second commandment which is to love God with all our heart, soul, strength, and mind. We do this through loving the people around us: husbands, wives, children, neighbors, co-workers, and anyone whom we meet in our daily activities. All too often Lent can easily slip into a self-centered time if we focus too much on ourselves such as people sometimes comment, *our* prayer, *our* confession, *our* fasting, and *our* almsgiving. Too much emphasis is placed on us and not God!

However, if we pay close attention to the Lenten prayers, hymns, and scripture readings we quickly realize that Lent is a time when we should put greater emphasis on others rather than on ourselves as we literally lay down our life for our neighbor. The last reading before the beginning of Great Lent is a good example. This particular reading is from Matthew 25:31-46. We hear about the King separating the sheep from the goats. The sheep are the ones who cared for the sick and suffering, clothed the naked, fed the hungry, and sheltered the homeless. The goats were the ones who did not. In other words, we learn that true Christian love is open, expansive, and directed towards other people. If we do not love other people then we will reap judgment as we hear in the gospel lesson. The Apostle Paul reminds us of love his first letter to the Corinthians, "love is patient and kind, love is not jealous or boastful, it is not arrogant or rude. Love does not insist on its own way; it is not irritable or resentful; it does not rejoice at wrong, but rejoices in the right. Love began all things, believes all things, hopes all things, endures all things" (1 Corinthians 13:4-7). We become more Christ like when we love other people. Throughout the season of Great Lent we are given numerous examples of love, which is taught to us through the scriptures,

---

1.   See Thomas Hopko *The Lenten Spring* (Crestwood, NY: St. Vladimir's Seminary Press, 1998)

prayers, and hymns during the preparatory Sundays of Lent and continue through Great Lent and Holy Week.

The Preparatory Sundays

The Church prepares us for Great Lent through a series of five pre-Lenten or pre-paratory Sundays: the Sunday of Zachaeus, the Publican and the Pharisee, the Prodigal Son, the Last Judgment, and Forgiveness Sunday. On these particular Sundays we hear a series of gospel readings that speak about repentance, forgive-ness, prayer, and love. Each gospel reading takes us one step closer to Great Lent.

The first three preparatory Sunday's include scripture lessons from the gospel of Luke while the last two Sunday's have readings from Matthew; Matthew 25:31-46 and Matthew 6:14-21 respectively. The first Sunday, while not techni-cally one of the preparatory Sundays, is called Zachaeus Sunday. On this day we hear about Zachaeus the tax collector who climbs a sycamore tree in order to see Jesus who is coming by the village. Jesus commands Zachaeus to come down from the tree because, "salvation has come to this house, since he also is a son of Abraham. For the Son of man came to seek and save the lost" (Luke 19:9). This theme of seeking and saving the lost is mentioned quite often in scripture espe-cially in the gospel of John where Jesus refers to himself as the good shepherd who not only lays down his life for his sheep, but who also leaves the 99 in search for the one sheep who is lost. Jesus comes to Zachaeus inviting him back to the community of faith, restoring him to the community.

The following week which is the first preparatory Sunday of Great Lent, we hear about the Prodigal Son who requests that he receive his inheritance from his father, leaves his home, squanders all of his inheritance, and then decides to return home in order to ask his father's forgiveness. However, before returning home, his father runs outside in order to greet him and welcomes him back. The father hosts a large banquet for his son because he was lost but now is found. Meanwhile, the father's eldest son, the one who remained home while his younger brother left, complains because his father did not give him a party. Luke tells us that during the younger brother's self-exile, the older brother stayed at home being a faithful son. However, despite the fact that he remained at home, he was very jealous that his father treated his younger brother in a special way. However, his father reminds him that during this time the older brother truly remained faithful, but his other son who was once lost is now found, who was once dead, is now alive.

Next we hear about the Publican and the Pharisee. We now turn to the gospel of Luke where we encounter a publican, which is another name for a tax collector, who is found praying in the Temple. The only prayer that he can utter is, "God, be merciful to me a sinner"; he is found standing by himself with his head bowed down (Luke 18:13). Off to the side is the Pharisee, a member of the Jewish ruling class, a true elder in his community, who is also found praying. However, his prayer is directed inwards, boasting about his accomplishments, fasting twice per week, giving alms, and most importantly, that he is not like this publican. At the end of this parable Jesus tells us that those who exalt themselves will be humbled and those who humble themselves will be exalted.

The fourth preparatory Sunday is called Judgment Sunday. The gospel reading for this Sunday is from Matthew 25:31-46 which is the story of the sheep and the goats. Jesus teaches his disciples about the future judgment and uses the imagery of a King who has to separate his sheep from the goats. Today, we hear about visiting the sick, feeding the hungry, clothing the naked, and visiting those in prison. These themes are repeated four times in this long lesson, which is a way to remind us that these things are very important in our life and will be the basis for our judgment. The Lord will ask each one of us, did we love our neighbor? When we show love to the neighbor we are actually showing love to God.

The final preparatory Sunday is called Forgiveness Sunday. This Sunday is also the last Sunday before Great Lent begins. Compared with the previous gospel lessons, this particular reading, a section from the Sermon on the Mount, is quite short. Jesus is on top of a mountain teaching his disciples and the crowds about prayer, fasting, and almsgiving. The Sermon on the Mount is also where we find the Beatitudes which we hear about every Sunday, "Blessed are the meek for they shall inherit the earth, blessed are those who mourn" and so forth. The Beatitudes, together with other passages of scripture, remind us of our task at hand: to love God means to love our fellow neighbor no matter where we find them.

It is a common tradition in many Orthodox Churches, that following the Divine Liturgy on this day the Church celebrates the Vespers of Forgiveness immediately followed by the Rite of Forgiveness. People ask one another for forgiveness before entering into the Lenten fast. We are now in Lent. During the solemn Vesper service we hear the following hymns which are poetic expositions on the previous gospel lessons which we heard during the preparatory Sundays:

> The door of divine repentance has been opened
> Let us enter with fervor having cleansed our bodies
> Observing abstinence from foods and passions in obedience to Christ
> Who has called the whole world to His heavenly Kingdom

Offering to the Master of all this tithe of the year
That we may look with love upon His Holy Resurrection

The grace of the Lord has shone forth
The grace which illumines our souls
This is the acceptable time
The time of repentance is here
Let us put aside the works of darkness
Let us put on the armor of light
That passing though Lent as through a great sea
We may reach the third-day Resurrection of our Lord Jesus Christ
The savior of our souls

Let us begin the Fast with joy
Let us give ourselves to spiritual efforts
Let us cleanse our souls
Let us cleanse our flesh
Let us fast from passions as we fast from foods
Taking pleasure in the good works of the Spirit
And accomplishing them in love
That we may be made worthy to the passion of Christ our God
And His Holy Pascha
Rejoicing with spiritual joy.

(Stikhera for Forgiveness Sunday Vespers)

Lent is not supposed to be a gloomy or drab time of year. Very often it can easily turn into a dark or morbid time, or even worse, a time for fulfilling mere obligations of fasting, prayer, confession, and Church attendance, following the rules and regulations of the Church, without a real change of heart. Lent is not about following rules or regulations, but about repentance, a change of heart. The late Orthodox liturgical theologian Alexander Schmemann referred to Lent as the Lenten Spring, a new birth, where we turn away from the darkness of sin and once again turn back to God:

For many, if not for the majority of Orthodox Christians, Lent consists of a limited number of formal, predominately negative rules and prescriptions:

abstention from certain food, dancing, perhaps movies. Such is the degree of our alienation from the real spirit of the Church that is almost impossible for us to understand that there is "something else" in Lent-something without which all these prescriptions lose much of their meaning. This "something else" can beset be described as an "atmosphere", a "climate" into which one enters, as first of all a state of mind, soul, and spirit which for seven weeks permeates our entire life. Let us stress once more that the purpose of Lent is not to force on us a few formal obligations, but to "soften" our heart so that it may be open itself to the realities of the spirit, to experience the hidden "thirst and hunger" for communion with God.[2]

Schmemann clearly associates Lent with a time for openness and softness of heart, a time where we are reminded of the supreme act of love. This sentiment is not original with Schmemann, but goes back to the Old Testament literature. The book of Deuteronomy invites us to seek a heart of flesh rather than a heart of stone. A heart of flesh means that it is soft and pliable, ready for change. A heart of stone means that we have a hard heart unable to change and is not pliable. Seeking a soft heart and seeking a life of God also means that we will hopefully return to the scriptures since the Word of God is the food which nourishes us and leads us back on the narrow path to the Kingdom. We turn to the scriptures during Lent for guidance and direction hopefully returning back to them throughout the year.

The Lenten season includes an abundance of scripture readings from both the Old and New Testaments. On Saturdays and Sundays we hear from the epistle to the Hebrews and from the gospel of Mark. During the weekdays we hear from the Old Testament, specifically from Isaiah, Genesis, and Proverbs. These readings are reminders of God's love for his people which goes all the way back to the time of the first patriarchs Abraham, Isaac, Jacob, when we hear about the creation of the world, Noah and the flood, as well as God's covenant with Abraham.

We also hear about Israel's apostasy and turning away from God. The prophet Isaiah reminds us of our need for returning back to God because of our sinful actions, "Thus says the Lord: "keep justice and do righteousness, for soon my salvation will come, and my deliverance be revealed. Blessed is the man who does this, and the son of man who holds fast, who keeps the Sabbath, not profaning it, and keeps his hand from doing evil" (Isaiah 56:1-2).

You are encouraged to consult a Church liturgical calendar for the scripture readings for Great Lent. Take a few moments out of your hectic and busy life to

---

2.   Alexander Schmemann *Great Lent: Journey to Pascha* (Crestwood, NY: St. Vladimir's Seminary Press, 1996), p. 31

xvi   Let Us Attend

read and reflect on God's Word during this special time of year. Regularly reading and reflecting on the scriptures will feed both your head and your heart as we make our annual Lenten pilgrimage together.

There are many ways to read and study the scriptures. Several resources are mentioned in the bibliography in the end of this book as well as in the introductions to my other books. The reader may also want to consult resources that are included in the back of many Bibles such as a map of the biblical world, as well as biblical glossaries or dictionaries. There are also many online resources for scripture study. A life centered around the Word of God is a wonderful activity, one which will feed you throughout your life journey.

The Gospel of Mark

It is likely that the author of the gospel was Paul's travel companion, named John Mark. According to the book of Acts, Mark was the son of Mary who lived in Jerusalem, "When he realized this, he went to the house of Mary, the mother of John whose other name was Mark, where many were gathered together and were praying" (Acts 12:12). Later in that same chapter we see that Mark traveled with Saul, who later changed his name to Paul, as well as with Barnabas, Paul's other travel companion, "and Barnabas and Saul returned from Jerusalem when they had fulfilled their mission, bringing with them John whose other name was Mark" (Acts 12:25).

According to Paul's epistle to Philemon we know that Mark was one of Paul's fellow workers and at the conclusion of this short letter we hear the following phrase, "Epaphas, my fellow prisoner in Christ Jesus, sends greetings to you, and so do Mark, Aristarchus, Demas, and Luke, my fellow workers" (Philemon 24) and "Aristarchus my fellow prisoner greets you, and Mark the cousin of Barnabas, concerning whom you have received instructions-if he comes to you receive him" (Colossians 4:10. See also 2 Timothy 4:11).

According to Irenaeus of Lyons, a bishop in the second century, reports that Mark was indeed the author of the gospel which is seen in the following statement from his famous treatise, *Against the Heresies*:

> Matthew also issued a written gospel among the Hebrews in their own dialect, while Peter and Paul were preaching in Rome, and laying the foundations of the Church. After their departure, Mark, the disciple and interpreter of Peter, did also hand down to us in writing what had been preached by Peter. Luke also, the companion of Paul, recorded in a book the gospel preached by him. Afterwards, John, the disciple of the Lord, who had also leaned upon his breast, did himself publish a gospel during his residence at Ephesus in Asia.

These have all declared to us that there is on God, creator of heaven and earth, announced by the law and the prophets; and one Christ, the Son of God. If any one does not agree to these truths, he despises the companions of the Lord, he despises Christ himself." (*Against Heresies* 3.2)

Irenaeus is one of our earliest sources who demarcated a four-fold gospel. He likens the four gospels to the four ends of the world; north, south, east, and west as well as four streams flowing from the one river which is Christ himself. Irenaeus was arguing vehemently against many heretical Christians who did not accept the gospels as the true Word of God nor did they acknowledge Jesus' true suffering and death on the cross. He is one of the defenders of our four gospel canon.

The gospel of Mark is also one of the synoptic gospels. The synoptic gospels are Matthew, Mark, and Luke. They are called synoptic which is derived from two Greek words that mean "seen together." The synoptic gospels share similar teachings, parables, and miracles such as Jesus walking on the water, the multiplication of loaves and fishes, as well as the other teachings and parables. If Matthew, Mark, and Luke are seen together side-by side many of the stories are either identical or very similar to one another.

Of the three synoptic gospels, Mark is the shortest with only sixteen chapters. Matthew is the longest with twenty-eight chapters and Luke is in the middle with twenty-four chapters. Even thought Mark is the shortest of the three, he does include a lot of information about Jesus and his ministry in a very short space. Most scholars have agreed that Mark was one of the earliest gospels written, later followed by Luke, John, and Matthew.

According to the Orthodox Christian lectionary the gospel of Mark is read on the weekends during Great Lent, on the feast of the Myrhhbearing Women which is celebrated on the second Sunday following Pascha (Easter), the weeks following the feast of Epiphany, as well as during the weeks following the feast of the Dormition of the Holy Theotokos in August. Mark's memory is commemorated and celebrated in the Church on April 25.

The sheer power of his gospel begins in the opening verses as we encounter the preaching of John the Baptist and his universal call to repentance:

The beginning of the gospel of Jesus Christ, the Son of God. As it is written in Isaiah the prophet, "Behold I send my messenger before thy face, who shall prepare thy way; the voice of one crying in the wilderness: prepare the way of the Lord, make his paths straight." John the Baptizer appeared in the wilderness, preaching a baptism of repentance for the forgiveness of sins. And there went out to him all the country of Judea, and all the people of Jerusalem; and they were baptized by him in the river Jordan, confession their sins (Mark 1:1-5).

The gospel begins very abruptly as we are introduced to John the Baptist. Mark does not tell us much about John other that he appeared sometime during his adult years preaching a gospel of repentance in the wilderness. John lived a very austere lifestyle eating only locusts and wild honey and wearing a shirt made from camel's hair. The gospel of Luke tells us that John's parents were Zechariah and Elizabeth, both holy and blameless believers who were advanced and years and could not have children. After some time Elizabeth was with child and gave birth to John. John is called the prophet and forerunner of our Lord since he came before Jesus, preparing his way, preaching of the kingdom of God. John's ascetic lifestyle combined with his preaching reveals his prophetic character as he lived a spartan life in the Judean desert. Mark begins his gospel citing a passage from the prophet Isaiah, "A voice cries: in the wilderness prepare the way of the Lord, make straight in the desert a highway for our God. Every valley shall be lifted up, and every mountain and hill made low; the uneven ground shall become level, and the rough places plain. And the glory of the Lord shall be revealed, and all flesh shall see it together, for the mouth of the Lord has spoken" (Isaiah 40:1-6).

We know that Jesus was not baptized by John, because he needed remission of sins, but so that his baptism would "fulfill all righteousness" (Matthew 3:15). However, while John was clearly baptizing and preaching the gospel of repentance, some of John's followers thought he himself was the Christ:

> "And this is the testimony of John, when the Jews sent priests and Levites from Jerusalem to ask him, "Who are you?" He confessed, he did not deny, but confessed, "I am not the Christ." And they asked him, "What then? Are you Elijah?" He said, "I am not." Are you the prophet?" And he answered, "No." They said to him then, "Who are you? Let us have an answer for those who sent us. What do you say about yourself?" He said, "I am the voice of the one crying in the wilderness, "Make straight the way of the Lord," as the prophet Isaiah said."(John 1:19-23)

John was a "voice of one crying in the desert." John called people to repentance, inviting them to return back to God. John's ministry reminded the Israelites to turn back to God which was similar to that of the prophet Isaiah. Isaiah told the Israelites to stop worshipping false gods and return to the one true living God, the God of Abraham, Isaac, and Jacob. However, the Israelites, like us, preferred to worship false gods and idols, "Their land is filled with idols; they bow down to the work of their hands, to what their own fingers have made" (Isaiah 2:8). John appeared as a voice in the wilderness, as another Isaiah, to ultimately prepare the way for Jesus. However, John, like most of the prophets, was persecuted for his preaching:

> At that time Herod the tetrarch heard about the fame of Jesus; and he said to his servants, "this is John the Baptist, he has been raised from the dead; that is why these powers are at work in him." For Herod had seized John and bound him and put him in prison, for the sake of Herodias, his brother Philip's wife, because John said to him, "it is not lawful for you to have her." And though he wanted to put him to death, he feared the people, because they held him to be a prophet. But when Herod's birthday came, the daughter of Herodias danced before the company, and pleased Herod, so that he promised an oath to give her whatever she might ask. Prompted by her mother, she said, "Give me the head of John the Baptist here on a platter." And the king was sorry; but because of his oaths and his guests he commanded it to be given; he sent and had John beheaded in the prison, and his head had was brought on a platter and given to the girl, and she brought it to her mother. And his disciples came, and took the body and buried it; and they went and told Jesus (Matthew 14:1-12).

Even in John's tragic death, he was a forerunner of the death of Jesus. John the Baptist reminds us to hold fast to the message of repentance. The word repent comes from the Greek word "metanoia" which literally means to have ones mind changed. Repentance is not an activity that we strive for during Great Lent, but rather, it is an activity which we strive for during our entire lifetime. To repent means to wake up out of our spiritual slumber and laziness and have a mind like Christ which is forgiving, merciful, loving, kind, and peaceful which we also see in various gospel readings in the scriptures such as the Samarian woman at the well, the Prodigal Son, and the Publican and the Pharisee. These lessons are constant reminders for us to return back to the Lord each and every day, struggling with our temptations and sins, seeking to follow Jesus on the narrow path to the Kingdom, as we hear towards the end of the prophet Isaiah, "Arise, shine, for your light has come, and the glory of the Lord has risen upon you. For behold, darkness shall cover the earth, and thick darkness the peoples; but the Lord will arise upon you, and his glory will be seen upon you. And nations will come to your light, and kings to the brightness of your rising" (Isaiah 60:1-3).

The Church reminds us to keep watchful and remain alert. During the Divine Liturgy we often hear the phrase, "Let us attend", which is also the title of this book. When we hear these three words we are reminded to wake up and hear God speaking to us. These words are said throughout the Liturgy, by either the deacon or priest, and especially before the reading of the scriptures, namely the epistle and gospel. Every time you hear "Let us attend" pay close attention to what is being said following these words. We remain alert because when God speaks to us it is a holy and important occasion. The reading of the scriptures followed by the sermon is a very special time. Be sure to be attentive to what the priest is saying because he is proclaiming the Word of God for the faith community and this word leads to repentance.

How To Use This Book

Let Us Attend is the fifth book in a series of lectionary studies on scripture. These easy to read books are marketed towards a general audience who are interested in learning more about the scriptures, especially in a parish setting. When the entire Church is reading and reflecting on the scriptures the entire Church is being built up and vivified.

This book can be used in a variety of ways, for personal or group Bible study or for sermon preparations. For personal or group Bible study the reader is first asked to read the gospel passage in Mark which corresponds to the appropriate chapter in *Let Us Attend*. Each chapter in *Let Us Attend* provides not only a reflection on the gospel lesson but also includes many scriptural references to other parts of the Bible such as the writings of the Apostle Paul and passages from the Old Testament. The reader is encouraged to read these additional scriptural references as well. After reading both the gospel lesson and the reflection in *Let Us Attend*, spend some time thinking about what you just read. What is Mark telling his readers? How can I apply these words to my life today? How can these words inspire me today? Very often a particular word, phrase, or image will come to you as you read the Bible. Take time to reflect on these words or phrases. If you are in a group Bible study, take time to share what you learned with others in the group. Other people may or may not have the same understanding of the lesson as you did.

Oftentimes these group discussions can be very fruitful and life-giving. It is always good to begin and end your scripture study with a prayer. You can use the Lord's Prayer as well as the prayer that is found at the beginning of this book which is from the Divine Liturgy of St. John Chrysostom. This prayer is a constant reminder that we need to not only hear the words of the scripture, but also live by them! When we are reading scripture, whether individually or in a group setting, we are being fed and nourished by Jesus Christ, the Word of God.

Also included in the appendix of this book are three sermons and reflections on the scripture by three Fathers of the Church: Augustine, Ephrem the Syrian, and John Chrysostom. There are very few full scriptural commentaries on the gospel of Mark from the Church Fathers. Therefore, I have included sermons that have parallel passages in either Matthew or Luke. Likewise, Ephrem's sermon on repentance is a beautiful poetic reflection on the Christian life. The reader is encouraged to read these sermons as well since they will provide much "food for thought" for our Lenten season. The Fathers were well versed in the scriptures, feeding both themselves and their flocks with the Word of God through preaching, teaching, and spiritual formation.

This book has been a labor of love and could not have been written without the love and support of my wife Taisia and my daughters Hannah and Emma; to them much is owed. Likewise, my parishioners at Nativity of the Holy Virgin in Charlotte, NC have heard parts of this book in sermons or in informal conversations. Unknown to them they became the fertile soil that gave birth to this series of lectionary studies books on scripture. I am grateful to them all. Finally, this book is dedicated to my friend and colleague, Father Stephen J. Hrycyniak who introduced me to the publishing world, a gift more than silver and gold. His continued support, encouragement, and inspiration is truly lifegiving.

1

Jesus' Ministry in Galilee
(Mark 1:35-44)

The grace has shown forth, O Lord
The grace which illumines our soul.
This is the acceptable time!
This is the time of repentance!
Let us lay aside all the works of darkness
And put on the armour of light
That passing through the fast as through a great sea
We may reach the resurrection on the third day
Of our Lord Jesus Christ, the Savior, of our souls
(Apostikha for Forgiveness Sunday)

When reading the gospel of Mark we see that Mark cultivates a sense of urgency in Jesus' ministry. Jesus is always on the move. Throughout the gospel we come across the word "immediately" over and over again emphasizing that Jesus is on a mission. Jesus must preach the gospel of the Kingdom and there is no time to waste! It is this deep sense of immediacy in which we encounter in today's gospel lesson.

Prior to today's reading Mark tells us that Jesus performed a series of three miracles: the cleansing of the demoniac in the synagogue (Mark 1:21-27), the healing of Peter's mother-in-law (Mark 1:29-31), and then the healing of a multitude of people who were demon possessed (Mark 1:32-34). These miracles all occur in the first chapter of Mark. These miracles are in a series of three. Throughout the gospel of Mark we will encounter this series or set of three again, three sets of teachings, three sets of miracles, and then three times Jesus predicts his own suffering and trials as he reminds his disciples to remain faithful.

Immediately following the series of these three miracles Jesus retires to a quiet place by himself to pray. We know from the other gospels that Jesus often went away by himself alone to pray, "Then he made the disciples get into the boat and go before him to the other side, while he dismissed the crowds. And after he had dismissed the crowds, he went up on the mountain by himself to pray (Matthew 14:23). We have a similar statement in the gospel of Luke, "In these days he went out to the mountain to pray; and all night he continued in prayer to God" (Luke 6:12). In the garden of Gethsamane Jesus also prayed to God the Father for strength during a very difficult time, "Father, if thou art willing, remove this cup from me, nevertheless, not my will, but thine be done. And when he rose from prayer, he came to the disciples and found them sleeping for sorrow, and he said to them, "why do you sleep? Rise and pray that you may not enter into temptation" (Luke 22:42-46).

However, Jesus is not alone very long. Simon Peter comes to get him since many people are looking for Jesus. Jesus was very popular with the general population in the area and we are told that many onlookers that witnessed his miracles and heard Jesus teaching. Presumably these crowds were following Jesus and his disciples for a while. Jesus responds to Peter by saying, "Let us go on to the next towns that I may preach there also; for this is why I came out." And he went throughout all Galilee, preaching in their synagogues and casting out demons" (Mark 1:38-39).

The Galilee area is where Jesus spent most of his time, preaching and teaching the Kingdom and healing people and driving out demons as we see in several passages, "While he was in one of the cities, there came a man full of leprosy; and when he saw Jesus, he fell on his face and besought him, "Lord, if you will, you can make me clean." And he stretched out his hand and touched him saying, "I will; be clean." And immediately the leprosy left him" (Luke 5:12-13. See also 8:22-25, Matthew 4:35-41; Matthew 14:21-33, and Mark 6:45-52).

The Galilee area is also where the Sea of Galilee is located, one of the largest lakes in the area; it is approximately 13 miles long and 8 miles wide. Around the shore are several cities such as Tiberias that was constructed during the reign of Herod the Great and was dedicated in honor of the Roman Emperor, Tiberius Caesar, who was the adopted son and heir to the throne of the famous Augustus Caesar. Augustus Caesar was the Roman Emperor when Jesus was born (Luke 2:1). The Sea of Galilee is also referred to as the Sea of Genesseret, which is mentioned in the other gospels as well (Matthew 14:34, Mark 6:53, Luke 5:1).

Furthermore, the Galilee region was the home of the "nations" or the Gentiles, the non-Jewish people. Jesus came to both the Jews and the Gentiles bringing the good news of the kingdom as we hear in the prophet Isaiah, "The land of Zebulun and the land of Naphtali, toward the sea, across the Jordan, Galilee of the Gentiles—the people who sat in darkness have seen a great light, and for those who sat in the region and shadow of death light has dawned" (Isaiah 9:1-2). Here Isaiah speaks about the messiah coming to the Gentiles in the area of the Galilee. We see a similar statement much later in the book of Isaiah, "It is too light a thing that you should be my servant to raise up the tribes of Jacob and to restore the preserved of Israel; I will give you as a light to the nations, that my salvation may reach to the end of the earth" (Isaiah 49:6-7).

In order to get to the Galilee area one must cross over the Jordan River, the famous river in Palestine where Jesus was baptized and where Joshua and the Israelites crossed over in order to get to the promised land. The Jordan river flows from north to south and has been a major river and place for pilgrimage for centuries. It is across the Jordan River, in the area of the Gentiles, where Jesus preached the gospel and devoted much time to his healing and teaching ministry.

The preaching of the gospel is directly associated with healing. Today's lesson tells us that a leper comes to Jesus in order to seek healing. In the ancient world leprosy was considered a very serious disease and was cause for being shunned from the community since it was a highly contagious disease and often caused an early death. Leper colonies were found near cities, but certainly outside the city walls or gates. Of all the diseases and maladies during the time of Jesus, leprosy was considered among the most terrible. We find details regarding leprosy in the Book of Leviticus:

> But if there is on the bald head or the bald forehead a reddish-white diseased spot, it is leprosy breaking out on his bald head or his bald forehead. Then the priest shall examine him, and if the diseased swelling is reddish-white on his bald head or on his bald forehead, like the appearance of leprosy in the skin of the body he is a leprous man, he is unclean; the priest must pronounce him unclean; his disease is on his head. The leper who has the disease shall wear torn clothes and let the hair of his head hang loose, and he shall cover his upper lip and cry, "unclean, unclean." He shall remain unclean as long as he has the disease; he is unclean: he shall dwell alone in the habitation of the camp. (Leviticus 13:42-46)

The text continues at great length discussing the types of clothes that the leper should wear as well as the various examinations that have to be undertaken by the priest. Leprosy was a disease that required extreme measures in order not to contaminate the rest of the community.

On one level this miracle seems very straight forward. A leper comes seeking healing from Jesus and he is healed from his leprosy. However, we have to keep in mind that Jesus is also in a non-Jewish area, an area of social outsiders. This makes the miracle even more powerful when we realize that Jesus goes out into the Gentile area and cures a man from his leprosy. Furthermore, the Jews believed that only God could heal lepers. In 2 Kings 5 the military commander named Naaman contacted leprosy. He went to the prophet Elisha asking for help and Elisha told him to go and wash himself in the Jordan River seven times and then he would be cleansed of his disease. Naaman did so and was cleansed and his flesh "was restored and became clean like a boy" (2 Kings 5:14). Lepers were shunned by the surrounding community and therefore, they had to subsist purely on donations and the kindness of other people for their survival.

Here we see Jesus actually touching the man because Jesus had "pity" on him. One could imagine the people's reaction to Jesus actually touching a man with leprosy because to do would defile a person and make them ritually unclean. Jesus also puts himself at risk by touching this disease man since the man was highly contagious. Jesus tells the man, "see that you say nothing to any one, but go, show yourself to the priest, and offer for your cleansing what Moses commanded, for a proof to the people" (Mark 1:44).

In order to find out what Jesus meant we have to go back to the book of Leviticus where we find an extensive "to do" list in case someone contracted an infectious disease. The religious rituals are numerous including the offering two live birds, obtaining twigs of hyssop, gathering some cedar wood, and purchasing two lambs and grain for a cereal offering. Additionally, the leper had to make several ritual baths and shave off all body hair before re-entering the community (Leviticus 14:1-32 and 13:49). This intricate and extensive procedure shows us that the culture and society wanted to make sure that the former leper would not contaminate the rest of the community with their leprosy. Likewise, the extensive notes about religious purification rites shows the very material ways in which the Jews envisioned their worship, which included animals, birds, and grains.

After the leper was cleansed Jesus tells him not tell anyone about the miracle. Yet the man goes and does exactly the opposite—he tells everyone what Jesus had done for him! A similar reaction is echoed in the gospel of John when the Samaritan woman goes out and tells the other Samaritans everything that Jesus told her (John 4:39-42). But why would Jesus want to keep this miracle a secret? After all, the man with leprosy was considered a social outcast in his community and was basically condemned to live a life of isolation, reduced to begging for food and money, and most likely experience an early death. The healing of the man is a cause for rejoicing.

Many people sought out Jesus because they wanted to see his earthly power and authority. After Jesus multiplies the loaves and fishes as recalled in the gospel of John, Jesus goes away quietly and hides by himself because the people want to make him a king (John 6:15). People often misunderstood Jesus' power, focusing on the immediate results while not realizing that the miracle directed them towards the Kingdom of God. Many people in the crowds were blinded and did not see Jesus' power as the Son of God.

This is not too much different from today where people always want to see a miracle, especially those performed by television evangelists in their Hollywood fashion with the smells and bells of miraculous power. Nightly media programs occasionally report of a person having a miraculous vision of Jesus in a taco shell or in a store window. Yet these stories come and go over time, they are somewhat of a fad. However, when Jesus performed miracles it was not for the sake of performing miracles as such, but that God's power should be revealed in the proclamation of the gospel. The miracle, whether calming a storm, healing a leper, or driving out demons always points to the Kingdom of God and the power of God in this world, especially over the darkness.

2

The Healing of the Paralytic (Mark 2:1-12)

Let us begin the fast with joy!
Let us prepare ourselves for spiritual efforts!
Let us cleanse our soul and cleanse our flesh!
Let us abstain from every passion as we abstain from food!
Let us rejoice in virtues of the spirit and fulfill them in love!
That we may all see the passion of Christ our God
And rejoice in the spirit as the holy Pascha!
(Stikhera for "Lord I Call" Forgiveness Vespers)

On this first Sunday of Lent we are presented with a miracle story which is also recounted in both the gospel of Luke 5:18-26 and Matthew 9:2-8. Mark tells us that that Jesus was in a house in Capernaum and was "preaching the word" to them. Capernaum was located on the north shore of the Sea of Galilee and it was one of the bases from which Jesus preached and ministered to the people. The gospel of Matthew says that Capernaum was Jesus' "own city" (Matthew 9:1). Furthermore, Capernaum is also where the centurion's servant was healed, where Jesus taught about the payment of the Temple tax, and where he had a discussion with James and John about who was the greatest disciple. The gospel of John tells us that it was near Capernaum, where Jesus multiplied the loaves and fishes (John 6:1-15). Capernaum was a perfect location to serve as a center for Jesus' ministry. The area included a mix of both Jew and Gentile and since the city was on the shore of a very large lake, there would have been a variety of merchants, sailors, and business people around. When reading the Book of Acts as well as Paul's epistles we also see that Paul used port cities as a base camp for his ministry, especially Ephesus and Corinth which had multiple ports.

6

Mark continues his gospel lesson telling us that while he was in a house preaching there were so many people that there were many standing outside in order to hear him preach. As Jesus was preaching the word to them, four men brought their paralyzed friend to the house, but because there were so may people present they could not enter. So they went ontop of the house and cut a section out of the roof in order to let down their friend down into the center of the house. During this time many houses had flat roofs so that people could use the space as a seating or resting area, very much like our front porches or backyard patios.

When Jesus saw these men and their determination to help their friend, Jesus said, "My son, your sins are forgiven" (Mark 2:5). In antiquity it was commonly thought that ones sins, whether paralysis or some other disease, was a result of sin. In the gospel of John Jesus encounters a man blind from birth and Jesus' disciples ask him, "Rabbi, who sinned, this man or his parents, that he was born blind?" Jesus answered, "It was not that this man sinned, or his parents, but that the works of God might be made manifest in him" (John 9:2-3). In other words, this man's blindness was not a result of a particular sin that he or his family committed, but that his blindness allowed Jesus to reveal his glory as the Son of God. A similar understanding of sin and ailments is echoed in the book of Exodus as God tells Moses, "You shall not worship them, for I the Lord God am a jealous God, punishing the children the sin of the fathers the third and fourth generation of those who hate me, but showing love to a thousand generations who love me and keep my commandments" (Exodus 20:5).

In today's lesson we also see that the Jewish leaders question Jesus' healing powers. They accuse Jesus of blasphemy because he forgave the man's sins. According to the Old Testament, blaspheming against God was a terrible transgression that warranted death by stoning, "He who blasphemes the name of the Lord shall be put to death; all the congregation shall stone him; the sojourner as well as the native, when he blasphemes the Name, shall be put to death" (Leviticus 24:16). Furthermore, to blaspheme the Lord also meant to discount God's promise of salvation, "Ah, sinful nation, a people laden with iniquity offspring of evildoers, sons who deal corruptly! They have forsaken the Lord, they have despised the Holy One of Israel, they are utterly estranged" (Isaiah 1:4, 5:25, Numbers 14:11). The Jewish leaders question Jesus' authority because they acknowledge that only God can forgive sins, they do not understand or accept the fact that Jesus is the messiah sent by God to forgive sins, to heal the blind and the lame, and to bring God's promise of salvation through the preaching of the gospel of the kingdom. After all, the Jewish leaders read scripture and in the prophet

Isaiah they understood that only God could forgive sins, "I, I am He who blots out your transgressions for my own sake, and I will not remember you sins" (Isaiah 43:25). The Jews were thinking that if only God could forgive sins then how could this earthly person, Jesus of Nazareth, the son of Joseph and Mary forgive sins? They see Jesus breaking the commandments, which is unthinkable according to the Law; Jesus heals on the Sabbath, spends time with sinners and outcasts of society, and speaks with the authority of God himself!

Furthermore, in addition to the healing miracle, we learn that Jesus refers to himself as the "son of Man." Throughout the gospels we see that Jesus has many titles that are attributed to him by other people: prophet, king, Lord, rabbi, teacher, son of David, Son of God, and Son of Man, and so forth. The title "son of man" hearkens back to the book of Daniel where we see this term used in reference to human persons. Daniel has a vision of heaven, specifically of God's throne, "I saw in the night visions, and behold, with the clouds of heaven there came one like a son of Man, and he came to the Ancient of Days and was presented before him. And to him was given dominion and glory and kingdom, and all peoples, nations, and languages should serve him; his dominion is an everlasting dominion, which shall not pass away, and his kingdom one that shall not be destroyed" (Daniel 7:13-14). We also have a similar description in the opening verses of the Book of Revelation where on the island of Patmos, John receives a vision of God's heavenly throne room:

> Then I turned to see a voice that was speaking to me, and on turning, I saw seven golden lampstands, and in the midst of the lampstands one like a son of man, clothed with a long robe and with a golden girdle round his breast; his head and his hair were white wool, white as snow; his eyes were like burnished bronze, refined as in a furnace, and his voice was like the sound of many waters; in his right hand he held seven stars, from his mouth issued a sharp two-edged sword, and his face was like the sun shining in full strength (Revelation 1:13-16).

The title "son of Man refers to the messiah of God who will receive all judgment, authority, and power from God the Father. This term also refers simply to the fact that the "son of Man" is a human person. We also see the phrase, the "son of Man" used in conjunction with the writings of the prophet Ezekiel. God speaks to Ezekiel and refers to Ezekiel as the Son of man, "And he said to me, "son of man, stand upon your feet, and I will speak with you." And when he spoke to me, the Spirit entered into me and set me upon my feet, and I heard him speaking to me. And he said to me, "son of man, I send you to the people of

Israel, to a nation of rebels, who have rebelled against me; they and their fathers have transgressed against me to this very day" (Ezekiel 2:1-3). This passage continues as the Lord reminds Ezekiel that Israel has truly rebelled against God and God wants Israel to return back to him. Therefore, we see that this term son of man refers both to Jesus' prophetic role as well as the fact that he is the son of man, a human person.

The short gospel lesson ends with a powerful statement about the true meaning of the healing of the paralytic which is expressed in the last verse, "so that they all were amazed and glorified God, saying, "We never saw anything like this!" (Mark 2:12. See also Matthew 9:8). This lesson ends with the people offering their prayer and praise to God, their worship as a result of encountering this miracle of the paralytic, which we also saw in the previous gospel lesson with the healing of the leper.

Throughout the scriptures we begin to realize that these miracles encourage faith. In the end of the second chapter of the gospel of John, after Jesus turns water into wine we read the following verses, "This, the first of his signs, Jesus did at Cana in Galilee, and manifested his glory; and his disciples believed in him" (John 2:11) which is also echoed at the end of the same gospel, "Now Jesus did many other signs in the presence of the disciples, which are not written in this book; but these are written that you may believe that Jesus is the Christ, the Son of God, and that believing you may have life in his name" (John 20:30-31. See also Acts 3:1-10). Jesus' miracles are not ends in themselves but point to something higher and greater than us. They point to God's power over creation.

3

The Calling of Levi
(Mark 2:14-17)

I have become the Prodigal Son
And having wasted my riches I perish now from hunger
Beneath thy protection I seek refuge, O loving Father:
Accept me as Thou hast accepted him
Make me a sharer at thy table that I may cry to Thee:
Before I perish utterly, save me O Lord
(Stickhera from Thursday of the Great Canon)

Today's reading is a continuation from the reading from last Sunday. Today's gospel reading is also found in Matthew 9:9-13 and Luke 5:27-32. Jesus went about the Sea of Galilee and was still preaching as he encountered Levi, the son of Alphaeus, who was sitting in the tax office or tax booth. The name Levi is a Jewish name that goes back to the Old Testament and sounds very similar to the name "Levites" who were the priestly class, who took care of the Jerusalem Temple. The reader might be familiar with the Book of Leviticus which describes, in great detail the many rites and rituals of the Temple.

Levi was sitting in the tax office because he was a tax collector. Only two tax collectors are specifically named in the New Testament: Levi and Zachaeus. Zachaeus is mentioned in Luke 19:1-19 which is the gospel reading for the Sunday just prior to the beginning of Great Lent. Jesus is walking in Jericho and upon looking up he notices Zachaeus in a sycamore tree. Jesus tells Zachaeus to come down because "salvation has come to this house, since he also is a son of Abraham. For the son of man came to seek and save the lost." Zachaeus hosts Jesus at a dinner and confesses that he will be generous with his money and will no longer commit any wrongdoing.

The reader also might be familiar with the parable of the Publican and the Pharisee which is also mentioned in the gospel of Luke, specifically Luke 18:9-14. Two men were praying in the Temple in Jerusalem, one was a Pharisee. Pharisees were among the leaders of the Jewish people and were well versed in the Old Testament Law and statutes. The other person in the parable was a Publican, another name for tax collector. However, this man does not have a proper name such as Zachaeus, we only know that he is sorry for his sins and prays "God, be merciful to me a sinner."

Tax collection was an important job for the Roman government. The Roman's had a highly structured tax system whereby they collected taxes in order to maintain their empire which included a well-equipped military force, excellent road, sewer, and aqueduct systems, as well as other building projects. Every Roman city also included large buildings, theaters, market places, coliseums, and amphitheaters. Ephesus, which has been renamed Kusadasi and is on the west coast of Turkey, had a stadium that could seat over 100,000 people. Many of these ancient buildings and roads can be seen throughout Europe and the Middle East and are major tourist sites even to this day.

Mark mentions that Levi was tax collector, but his name is a Jewish name which means that he was a Jew who was working for the Roman government. In the eyes of his friends he most likely would be seen as a traitor, or at least as a collaborator with the Romans, very much like the Vichy government in World War II France who were looked down upon by many of the French population for not resisting the Nazi government.

The tax collectors not only collected the tax like our national Internal Revenue Service, but they collected a percentage as a commission for themselves. Then, as now, tax collectors are not well liked! Yet, even though tax collectors were not the most popular people in those times, Jesus notices Levi in the tax booth and invites him to come and "Follow me." And he rose and followed him" (Mark 2:14). The brevity of their meeting and the response by Levi is astounding. Later we know that Levi's name was changed to Matthew which is a Greek word meaning "gift of God." Levi leaves behind his former way of life, collecting taxes and working for the Romans, and follows Jesus.

In addition to Levi we know that Jesus disciples as well. Earlier in Mark 1:16 we see Jesus calling his disciples, "And passing along by the Sea of Galilee, he saw Simon and Andrew the brother of Simon casting a net in the sea; for they were fishermen. And Jesus said to them, "Follow me and I will make you become fishers of men." And immediately they left their nets and followed him. And going on a little father, he saw James the son of Zebedee and John his brother, who were in their boat mending their nets. And immediately he called them; and they left their father Zebedee in the boat with the hired servants, and followed him" (Mark 1:16-20, Matthew 4:18-22, Luke 5:1-11, John 1:35-42). Jesus sent his disciples out into the world to fulfill his ministry of preaching, teaching, and healing, "And he appointed twelve to be with him, and to be sent out to preach and have authority to cast out demons (Mark 3:13). The gospel of Matthew tells us that Jesus gave them detailed instructions about ministry such as living a simple life, speaking the truth in love, and to be wise as serpents and innocent as doves (Matthew 10).

In addition to the disciples mentioned in Mark chapter two, we also know that Jesus had other disciples and followers: Philip and Bartholomew, Thomas, Judas Iscariot, and Simon from Canaan. The gospel of John also mentions Nathaniel (John 1:47-49). Jesus also had women followers such as Mary his mother, Mary Magdalene, Joanna, Mary the mother of James, and Suzanna (Luke 23:10-12). Luke also tells us that besides the twelve disciples Jesus also had the seventy whom he sent out to minister and to preach the gospel.

These disciples came from all walks of life, many of the disciples were fisherman such Peter and Andrew, Matthew was a Jewish tax collector working for the Roman government, Mary Magdalene was said to have had several demons driven from her. In other words, Jesus certainly had a colorful following of characters as his friends. Many of his followers were considered either unclean or outside the realm of Jewish purity rules and regulations. The Jewish leaders question Jesus' choice of friends by asking, "Why does he eat with tax collectors and sinners? And when Jesus heard it he said to them, "Those who are well have no need of a physician, but those who are sick; I came not to call the righteous, but sinners" (Mark 2:16-17) which is similar to Jesus' words in Luke, "For the son of man came to seek and save the lost" (Luke 19:10). The word sin means to miss the mark or to get off track. Thus, if we sin we are not following the Lord but following our own false demons or idols which we have created for ourselves. Furthermore, if we are off the mark we are lost and therefore are the very ones whom Jesus comes to save.

Throughout the gospels Jesus is seen with many people whom the society and culture would consider outcasts and unclean. He spends time with Samaritans who were considered half-breeds, part Jewish and part Gentile, who were unworthy to live with the other Jewish people; lepers who were looked down upon because of their highly contagious disease, tax collectors, former prostitutes and harlots, and simple fishermen.

The fact that Jesus also had women followers was also counter-cultural given the fact that rabbis did not associate with persons of the opposite gender, especially in private settings. Therefore the fact that a woman washed Jesus feet with her hair and his private meeting with the Samaritan Woman at Jacob's Well was not an ordinary activity in the ancient world. Jesus truly was a rebel, going against the social and religious customs of his day to show that God's ways are not man's ways and that God has a much bigger plan for humanity than we could ever imagine! Jesus' rebellion caused a great disturbance among the Jewish authorities as we see in today's gospel lesson.

While Jesus certainly spent time with Jewish leaders, we know that he spoke with a Jewish leader named Nicodemus, and he did attend worship in both the local synagogue and worshiped in the Temple in Jerusalem, most of his time was spent talking and eating with the outcasts of society. In many of the prayers of the Church Jesus is called the Physician of our souls. He is the doctor who comes to heal us of our diseases and maladies, bringing wholeness and healing. He calls the sick and the suffering, the diseased and the lame. Those who are righteous do not need such help.

The Apostle Paul echoes these words in his epistle to Timothy, "The saying is sure and worthy of full acceptance, that Jesus came into the world to save sinners. And I am the foremost of sinners; but I received mercy for this reason, that in me, as the foremost, Jesus Christ might display his perfect patience for an example to those who were to believe in him for eternal life" (1 Timothy 1:15). Paul's words are also repeated in the Divine Liturgy as we recite the prayer before Holy Communion by saying, "I believe O Lord and I confess that Thou art the Christ, the Son of the living God who came to save sinners of whom I am the first." Before receiving the very Body and Blood of Christ we have to acknowledge our unworthiness and sinfulness so that we do not make the mistake of somehow thinking that we are worthy or righteous enough to receive it. If we think that we are well we do not need Jesus and therefore do not need the Church. I hope that none of us would be so proud and arrogant to think that, otherwise, we are truly missing the mark and off the narrow path to the Kingdom.

Jesus ministered to the lowly, the poor, widows, orphans, homeless, diseased, marginalized, and meek. He called fishermen and tax collectors to join him in his proclamation of the Kingdom of God. It is up to us, like Levi, to drop what we are doing and follow him and hopefully he will invite us into his heavenly Kingdom.

4

Taking Up the Cross (Mark 8:34-9:1)

Before Thy cross

We bow down and worship O Master

And Thy resurrection we glorify

(Troparion for the Sunday of the Cross)

If you have read closely you will notice that the gospel readings during Lent are not in the same order as they appear in the gospel itself. In other words, the gospel readings during Lent are not read in a linear fashion starting with chapter one and then chapter two and so forth. On the first reading from Mark we started from chapter one. However, we then skipped to chapter eight. This is not uncommon. If you take a few moments and look at a liturgical calendar you will see that many readings are not read in a linear fashion, they often skip around. This is because the particular readings for a given day are assigned for a special purpose such as a reading for a special saint or feast day. Furthermore, as was noted in the introduction, part of the gospel of Mark is read during other seasons in the Church year such as following the feast of Epiphany and after the feast of the Dormition of the Theotokos. During Lent we are getting a small portion of the gospel stories. The reader is encouraged to read the entire gospel on their own in order to get a better flow of the text. Mark is the shortest of the four gospels and one could easily read the entire gospel in one sitting.

During last week's reading we encountered Jesus calling his disciples. This week we hear about the conditions for discipleship—what it means to be a disciple. Immediately prior to today's reading we read that Jesus speaks to his disciples and predicts the end, "And he began to teach them that the Son of man must suffer many things, and be rejected by the elders and the chief priests and the scribes, and be killed, and after three days rise again" (Mark 8:31). This is the second of

14

three predictions of Jesus' death, the other two are found in Mark 9:30-32 and Mark 10:33-34 respectively. The repetition of his end is intentional, it emphasizes that Jesus is identified with the suffering servant as we read in the prophet Isaiah:

> Surely he has borne our griefs and carried out sorrows; yet we esteemed him stricken, smitten by God and afflicted. But he was wounded for our transgressions, he was bruised for our iniquities; upon him was the chastisement that made us whole, and with his stripes we are healed. All we like sheep have gone astray; we have turned every one to his own way; and the Lord has laid on him the iniquity of us all. He was oppressed and afflicted, yet he opened not his mouth; like a lamb that is led to the slaughter, and like a sheep that before its shearers is dumb, so he opened not his mouth (Isaiah 53:4-7).

> The Lord God has given me the tongue of those who are taught, that I may know how to sustain with a word him that is weary. Morning by morning he wakens, he wakens my ear to hear those who are taught. The Lord God has opened my ear, and I was not rebellious, I turned not backward, I have my back to the smiters, and my cheeks to those who pulled on the beard; I hid not my face from shame and spitting (Isaiah 50:4-6).

> Behold, my servant shall prosper, he shall be exalted and lifted up, and shall be very high. As many were astonished at him, his appearance was so marred, beyond human semblance, and his form beyond that of the sons of men, so shall he startle many nations; kings shall shut their mouths because of him; for that which has not been told them they shall see, and that which they have not heard they shall understand (Isaiah 52:13-15).

The passages from Isaiah are also read on Holy Friday during Holy Week. Jesus is identified with the suffering servant, the one who will be offered up as a blameless sacrifice on behalf of the sins of the people. Isaiah speaks about one who will bear afflictions, who is marred beyond resemblance, and by whose stripes we are healed. This sentiment is echoed in the gospel of John as John reminds us that Jesus is the Lamb of God who takes away the sins of the world, a statement made by John the Baptist just prior to the beginning of Jesus' ministry (John 1:29-36). Towards the end of the gospel, we see that Jesus is crucified outside of Jerusalem on the same day that the Passover lambs are being slain for the annual Passover supper. The Passover was the Jewish holy day commemorating their salvation from Egypt and their bitter bondage to Pharoah and his court. At Passover the Jews remembered God's saving hand in their lives. This image of salvation and sacrifice is enhanced in Jesus' own life as the Lamb of God who truly takes upon himself the sins of the world.

When Jesus foretells the approaching end of his life, Peter, the chief disciple "rebuked" Jesus. To rebuke someone is to put them down with ones words, to castigate or berate them. Thus, Peter berates Jesus, the very son of God and goes against Jesus' entire teaching. In answer to Peter Jesus says, "Get behind me Satan! For you are not on the side of God, but of men" (Mark 8:33). These are very harsh words that come from Jesus. Nowhere else in scripture does Jesus call his own disciples "Satan." The word Satan is also translated as the word Devil which is derived from the Greek word diablos which means deceiver, divider, or liar. We find this term in the book of Job where Satan comes to God asking permission to harass Job in order to test him (Job 2:1-10). Jesus calls Peter a liar because Peter denies Jesus' own words that he is going to suffer and to die. Peter denies Jesus ministry as the suffering servant and wants him to live—-yet three times Jesus predicts that he will die!

Immediately after Jesus rebukes Peter he takes his disciples aside and tells them, together with the crowds, that whoever would be his disciple must deny himself, take up his cross, and follow Jesus (Mark 8:34). This instruction is also mentioned in both Matthew 16:24-28 and in Luke 9:23-27, but in slightly different ways:

> Then Jesus told his disciples "if any man would come after me, let him deny himself and take up his cross and follow me. For whoever would save his life will loose it, and whoever looses his life for my sake will find it. For what will it profit a man, if he gains the whole world and forfeits his life?

> And he said to them all, "If any man would come after me, let him deny himself, and take up his cross daily and follow me. For whoever would save his life will loose it; and whoever loses his life for me sake, he will save it. Fro what does it profit a man if he gains the whole world and loses or forfeits his soul?

Both readings are more or less similar, the main difference is that in Matthew Jesus directs his attention to the "disciples" while Luke tells us that Jesus directs his statement to "all" who were listening, both to the disciples and to the surrounding crowds. Furthermore, Luke also adds the word "daily" when Jesus says that his disciple must take up his cross "daily" which is a way of emphasizing every single day one must get up and take up the cross of Christ.

Taking up ones cross is also a very powerful statement because it is not only dying with Jesus but also requires suffering, self-denial, humility, and shame.

When we see someone wearing a cross on their neck or if we see a large crucifix on the wall of a Church we might not always remember that crucifixion was a very shameful and public death. Crucifixion was a common method of capital punishment which was reserved for common criminals, thieves, and non-Roman citizens. A few details concerning the crucifixion process are needed in order for us to have a better picture of how the cross is considered shameful.

A criminal who was condemned for crucifixion had to carry a large piece of wood which was the crossbar. Their hands were attached to the wooden beam by a heavy rope. The tall upright portion of the cross remained fixed in the ground. Crucifixions took place outside of the city walls as a reminder to visitors not to break the law, otherwise, they might wind up like the people hanging on the crosses. In our culture we have something similar when we see large billboards on the highways, warning about drunk driving or driving without a license or warnings about additional fines in work areas and so forth.

The condemned criminal was then beaten or as the gospels say, "scouraged" and then stripped naked, their hands were tied to the large horizontal piece which was the crossbar. Their bodies were then lifted high upon the vertical piece of wood and they were left to hang there until they died. Crucifixion was also a very painful way to die since the person was going to die from aphsyxian which is the lack of oxygen. This process took several hours. In the gospels we know that Jesus hung on the cross for at least three hours if not more (Mark 15:33). The legs were sometimes broken in order to hasten death since the person's legs would be helping to hold up their bodies in order to breath better. The gospels mention that the Roman soldiers broke the legs of the two thieves who were crucified with Jesus but not his because when they came to break his legs Jesus was already dead.

Crucifixion then was certainly a shameful way to die. It was public, violent, and humiliating. Yet Jesus tells his disciples that taking up ones cross is a sign of discipleship. We are constantly reminded of this theme in Church. Every time we make the sign of the cross over our bodies when we say our daily prayers we are reminded of our discipleship. When the priest blesses us with the sign of the cross we are reminded of our discipleship. Twice a year, on the feast of the Exaltation of the Cross on September 14 and during the third week of Great Lent, a small cross is decorated with flowers, placed in the middle of the Church, and kissed by the faithful. We are reminded of our discipleship. At the service of baptism a newly baptized child is given a cross to wear around their neck and they are anointed with holy chrism with the sign of the cross. They make their first procession around the baptismal font by walking with their sponsors behind the priest who holds a cross. They are reminded of their discipleship. A newly married couple makes their first

procession around the center icon in the Church walking behind the priest who car-
ries a cross. They are reminded of their discipleship. The cross is brought out on
Holy Friday for veneration. We are reminded of our discipleship.

Perhaps the cross is such a prominent part of our life that we have lost its
power. The Apostle Paul reminds us that the cross is truly powerful, "For the
word of the cross is folly to those who are perishing, but to us who are being
saved it is the power of God" and later on in the same passage Paul continues,
"For Jews demand signs and Greeks see wisdom, but we preach Christ crucified,
a stumbling block to Jews and folly to Gentiles, but to those who are called both
Jews and Greeks Christ the power of God and the wisdom of God" (1 Corinthians 1:11 and 1:22-25). Jesus' death on the cross seemed to be a sign of weakness to those who were watching, the crowds were shouting and deriding him
from below. They saw him cure illnesses, drive out demons, and walk on water,
but they saw his death as a sign of humiliation. Yet, Paul reminds us that the
cross is powerful in that Jesus became totally empty of his own human power and
strength and laid down his life for the sake of the world. His complete obedience
to God the Father is echoed in Paul's letter to the Philippians:

> Have this mind among yourselves which is yours in Christ Jesus, who though
> he was in the form of God, did not count equality with God a thing to be
> grasped, but emptied himself, taking the form of a servant, being born in the
> likeness of men. And being found in human form he humbled himself and
> became obedient unto death, even death on a cross. Therefore God has highly
> exalted him and bestowed on him the name which is above every name, that
> in the name of Jesus every knee should bow, in heaven and on earth and under
> the earth, and every tongue confess that Jesus Christ is Lord, to the glory of
> God the Father (Philippians 2:5-11).

Paul reminds us that God raised and exalted Jesus Christ but he could only do
so if Christ was completely obedient to him. Again, Jesus is seen as the suffering
servant, the one who bears the afflictions and pain of humanity in order to return
us to God the Father. Jesus' death on the cross brings unity to the universe, as he
himself says in the gospel of John, "when you have lifted up the Son of man, then
you will know that I am he, and that I can do nothing on my own authority but
speak thus as the Father taught me. And he who sent me is with me; he has not
left me alone, for I always do what is pleasing to him (John 8:27-30).

Sometimes symbols that are so common, such as the cross, are easily over-
looked and forgotten. Yet, during the third week of Great Lent we are reminded
that just as Jesus took up and carried his cross, so too, we are invited to do the

same. The gospel of Mark reminds us of our high calling as Jesus' disciples, that we are supposed to take up our cross, a symbol of humility, service, and obedience, and follows Christ. This is easier said then done because it goes against our human nature. Who wants to live a life of service, of lowliness, and being under obedience? Christians do!

5

The Healing of the Deaf Man (Mark 7:31-37)

O Lord and Master of my life

Take from me the Spirit of sloth, despair, lust of power, and idle talk

But rather give the spirit of chastity, humility, patience, and love to
   thy brother

Yea O Lord and King grant me to see my own sins and not to judge
   thy brother

For blessed art thou unto the ages of ages. Amen.

(Prayer of St. Ephraim of Syria)

As we continue reading the gospel of Mark we know that Jesus spends a lot of time healing people. We already saw how Jesus healed the paralytic and next week we will encounter Jesus healing the epileptic from his debilitating seizures. Today's reading also contains a healing miracle of a man who as both deaf and dumb which is also found in the gospel of Matthew 15:29-31. The mentioning of a double illness, the lack of speech and hearing, makes Jesus' miracle even more powerful since Jesus manifests his supreme power and authority over diseases and nature. In other words not only does Jesus heal this man from one illness, but two!

Just prior to today's gospel lesson we know that Jesus was in the area of Tyre and Sidon, two cities located on the farthest reaches of western Palestine, which are on the coast of the Mediterranean Sea. The cities are approximately 25 miles from one another and although they were populated by Jews, they were known for having a large Gentile population. Both Tyre and Sidon had numerous ports for shipping and marketing to other nations. The prophets proclaimed judgment against these cities not only for the injustices and corruption in them but also for exporting their false gods and idols over to Israel. Likewise, both Tyre and Sidon had an extensive slave trade which is mentioned by the prophet Amos, "Thus says the Lord: for three transgressions of Tyre, and for four, I will not revoke the punishment, because they delivered up a whole people to Edom, and did not remember the covenant of brotherhood. So I will send a fire upon the wall of Tyre, and it shall devour her strongholds" (Amos 1:9-10). The Old Testament generally mentions Tyre and Sidon together and usually not in a great light:

> Wail of ships of Tarshish, for Tyre is laid waste, without house or haven! From the land of Cyprus it is revealed to them. Be still, O inhabitants of the coast, O merchants of Sidon; your messengers passed over the sea and were on many waters; your revenue was the grain of Shihor, the harvest of the Nile; you were the merchant of the nations. Be ashamed, O Sidon, for the sea has spoken, the stronghold of the sea, saying; I have neither travailed nor given birth, I have neither reared young men nor brought up virgins." When the report comes to Egypt they will be in anguish over the report about Tyre (Isaiah 23:1-7).

The prophets were sent to these cities preaching repentance and the people did not respond. Therefore, God's wrath was going to come upon them. This seemingly small detail provide to us by Mark is important. Jesus is in the area of Tyre and Sidon, a Gentile area which is notorious for its paganism and rebellion against God. It is here within this area that Jesus performs a great miracle.

The people in the area brought Jesus a man who was both deaf and dumb seeking healing. Mark tells us that Jesus took the man aside privately to perform the miracle. While Mark does not tell us the reason why Jesus did this, it is likely, as we have seen throughout the gospel narrative, that Jesus does not want to draw unnecessary attention to himself, but rather, invites people to faith in the biblical God. After Jesus put his finger in the man's ear and put some spittle on the man's tongue the man's hearing and speech were restored. This miracle is reminiscent of the healing of the man born blind which is in the ninth chapter of the gospel of John. Jesus takes some soil from the ground and mixes it with his own spittle and anoints the man's eyes. Jesus then sends the man to the pool of Siloam to wash. The man's sight has returned and he comes back to Jesus. In the two miracle stories we see Jesus using ordinary natural material such as soil and some human spittle to restore peoples physical health.

The miracle is a fulfillment of Jesus' messianic ministry. The importance of healing the blind and the deaf are signs that the messiah has arrived which is echoed in the writings of the prophet Isaiah, "Then the eyes of the blind shall be opened, and the ears of the deaf unstopped; then shall the lame man leap like a hart, and the tongue of the dumb sing for joy. For waters shall break forth in the wilderness, and the streams in the desert; the burning sand shall become a pool, and the thirsty ground springs of water; the haunt of jackals shall become a swamp, the grass become reeds and rushes" (Isaiah 35:5-7).

This passage is also adapted in the gospel of Luke 4:32-33 where Jesus begins his ministry. Jesus stands up in the local synagogue and reads a portion of scripture from Isaiah, but from another passage, which speaks about preaching the good news to the poor, proclaiming release to the captives, and making the blind see, "The Spirit of the Lord is upon me, because he has anointed me to preach good news to the poor. He has sent me to proclaim release to the captives and recovering of sight to the blind, to set at liberty those who are oppressed, to proclaim the acceptable year of the Lord" (Luke 4:18-19. See also Isaiah 61:1-5). A few chapters later in the same gospel, Jesus sends out his disciples with the same ministry of preaching and healing, "And he called the twelve together and gave them power and authority over all demons and to cure diseases, and he sent them out to preach the kingdom of God and to heal" (Luke 9:1-2). In the book of Acts we also see the apostles continuing this same ministry of preaching the gospel and healing. In other words, the work of the Church is to continue Jesus' ministry in both word and deed until he returns again to judge the whole world.

Therefore, as ambassadors of the Kingdom, it is our vocation to fulfill Jesus' important ministry in our unique circumstance in our particular setting. As Jesus sent out his disciples to continue his ministry, so to we are supposed to continue his ministry as well. If we are members of this body of Christ, the Church, then our task is to increase and strengthen this body wherever we are with whomever is with us. This is also echoed in the petitions of the Divine Liturgy such as the following one, "Let us commend ourselves and each other and all our life unto Christ our God." Each and every day we are called to commend or commit ourselves as well as other members of our family and other members of the Church to Christ. We have to build up another and encourage one another every day. This of course is not an easy task, it may even seem impossible at times.

However, we cannot strengthen and encourage others if we are not ourselves being continually strengthened and encouraged, especially by the Word of God. In his epistle to the Romans, Paul tells them, "But how are men to call upon him in whom they have never believed? And how are they to believe in him of whom they have never heard? And how are they going to hear without a preacher? And how can men preach unless they are sent? As it is written, "How beautiful are the feet of those who preach good news!" (Romans 10:14-15). In other words before we share our faith in Christ we have to make sure that we know it and can pass it along to other people. We learn our faith by studying the Word of God and living out this Word in our lives. This may seem overwhelming, and it often is, but Jesus left us with the Holy Spirit to guide, inspire, sustain, and encourage us in our darkest and most difficult moments. At every Divine Liturgy we are reminded of this great gift of the Holy Spirit as we hear in the following prayers. The first one is chanted by the priest at the beginning of the Liturgy and the second one is a prayer just prior to the consecration of the gifts of bread and wine:

> O Heavenly King the comforter the Spirit of Truth
> Who art everywhere and fills all things
> Treasury of blessings and giver of life
> Come and abide in us, cleanse us from every impurity and save our souls O good One.
>
> Again we offer unto Thee this reasonable and bloodless worship, and ask Thee, and pray Thee and supplicate Thee: send down Thy Holy Spirit upon us and these gifts here offered

In these prayers we invoke the blessings of the Holy Spirit into our midst, as we begin the Liturgy we invite the Holy Spirit to cleanse us from our impurity, our sins and to inspire us to offer our prayer and worship to God. The second prayer, recited just prior to the consecration of the gifts of bread and wine, remind us that the Holy Spirit is not just sent to sanctify the gifts, but the entire faith community who are gathered together around the altar. Many people fail to hear the slight nuance in the prayer, they realize that the priest is invoking the Spirit on the gifts, but they forget that the priest is also invoking the Holy Spirit on them too! This is very important since the entire congregation is gathered around the table as a sign of our unity in love and faith in Jesus Christ. Hopefully every liturgy is a reminder of our high calling, our vocation, to serve the Lord in our life as we go about our daily routines at work, home, or school.

6

The Healing of the Epileptic Boy (Mark 9:17-31)

We have sinned
We have transgressed
We have done evil in thy sight
We have not kept or followed thy commandments
But reject us not utterly, O God of our Fathers
(7th Ode Great Canon of St. Andrew of Crete)

In today's reading we are presented with the final miracle in a series of three miracles. As was previously noted in the introduction, Mark uses a series or sequence of three throughout his gospel: three sets of miracles followed by a series of three teachings, and then three predictions of the end. Recently we encountered the healing of the mute and deaf man which was then followed by the account of Jesus' transfiguration on the mountain before his disciples Peter, James, and John; and then today's reading, the miracle about the demon possessed man. This series of three miracles reminds us of Jesus power and authority over the natural world, that not only is he a prophet, a teacher, or a miracle worker, but he is the very Son of God who calms the storm, drives out demons, and walks on water.

We know that there was a crowd that surrounded Jesus and then a heated discussion erupted. Mark does not provide us with many details, but we do know that the father's son had severe convulsions due to demonic possession. The gospel tells us that the demons wreaked havoc on this young boy which greatly disturbed his father. The father brought the boy to the disciples but they could not do anything to help them. Here again we see the disciples, Jesus' inner circle of friends, unable to fulfill their calling as disciples. Jesus publicly rebukes them by saying, "O faithless generation, how long am I to be with you? How long am I to bear with you? Bring him to me" (Mark 9:19). These are very strong words from Jesus; he calls them a "faithless generation" due to their lack of faith and trust. Jesus often speaks about having great faith and at one point in the gospel of Matthew, he describes faith using the image of a mustard seed, "I say to you, if you have faith as a grain of mustard seed, you will say to this mountain, "Move from here to there," and it will move; and nothing will be impossible to you" (Matthew 17:20-21).

However, here, in the gospel of Mark, Jesus berates his very own disciples for their lack of faith which is contrasted with the appearance of the father in the reading who has enough faith to come to Jesus in order to seek healing for his son. This theme of the lack of faith of Jesus' disciples contrasted with the strong faith of Gentiles or outsiders is seen throughout the gospel of Mark as well as the other three gospel accounts. Peter, the chief disciple lacks faith and sinks in the water as he was coming to Jesus. Then at the end of the gospel Peter denies that he even knows Jesus as Jesus was being condemned by the Sanhedrin, the Jewish court; Thomas doubts Jesus' resurrection, Nathaniel doubts that anything good can come out of Nazareth—Jesus' own village; and then on the way to the seaport of Caeserea-Philipi, James and John, the sons of Zebedee argue who will be the greatest in the Kingdom! Yet the gospels show us that even the demons know Jesus' true identity!

The father comes to Jesus making a confession of faith, he says, "I believe, help my unbelief!" (Mark 9:24). Several times the scriptures mention a confession of faith made by one of Jesus' followers. There are many people in the gospel who publicly acknowledge Jesus and his mission. The gospel of John opens with a confession made by Nathaniel as he tells Jesus, "Rabbi, you are the Son of God! You are the King of Israel" (John 1:49). This short confession includes several important aspects: rabbi, son of God, and King of Israel. Nathaniel calls Jesus a "rabbi" which denotes Jesus' teaching authority. The rabbi's were among the Jewish leaders who were well versed in the Old Testament and had extensive training in the Law. According to the book of Acts, the famous Rabbi Gamaliel in Jerusalem trained the Apostle Paul.

The terms "son of God" and "King of Israel" points to Jesus' kingship which is linked to his forefather David. The messiah was supposed to come from the royal lineage of David, and David was one of the greatest kings in the Old Testament. David also united both the northern kingdom of Israel as well as the southern kingdom of Judah. The savior was going to come from the house of David which is mentioned in the genealogy of Jesus, "The book of the genealogy of Jesus Christ, the son of David, the son of Abraham (Matthew 1:1).

Jesus is not just another religious teacher, but is the Son of God and the King of Israel. Towards the end of the same gospel, we find another confession of faith, one of the most important in all the scriptures. After the resurrection Jesus comes to Thomas who was absent at the previous post-resurrection sighting. The second time Jesus comes to his disciples Thomas exclaims that Jesus is "My Lord and My God" (John 20:28). This is the only place in the scriptures that Jesus is referred to as "God" which hearkens back earlier in the gospel where Jesus says that he is working and his Father is working which insights the crowd to want to kill him, "I and the Father are one. The Jews took up stones again to stone him" (John 10:30). A public affirmation of faith is important because is shows ones trust and faith. While the disciples seem to not understand Jesus' identity as the son of God, certainly the demons do. However, there are several instances in the gospel where the disciples make a confession of faith to show their allegiance and trust.

The end of the gospel lesson is very stark. Jesus and his disciples were going throughout the Galilee area and Jesus was teaching them that, "The son of Man will be delivered into the hands of men, and they will kill him; and when he is killed after three days he will rise" (Mark 9:31). This is one of several public statements about Jesus end. Each week during Lent we slowly come to terms that Jesus is slowly approaching his demise, he is going to his end.

Confessing that Jesus is our Lord and our God means that we publicly confess that among all the gods and lords in life, which there are many, we only worship one, who is Jesus Christ, the son of God. This exclamation of faith is expressed in a more formal manner in the Nicene Creed which we also recite or sing at the Divine Liturgy. Before we approach the altar table with the gifts of bread and wine we must confess before everyone that we worship the biblical God. We do this because we enter the Church with many idols and gods which we must let go; the god of materialism, the god of jealousy, the god of anger, the idol of pride, and so forth. Just as Moses slammed down the ten commandments on the golden calf of Baal on Mount Sinai, so too must we cast off the many false gods and idols in our life that control us.

If we do not confess that Jesus is the Christ the son of God, then we consume the gifts of bread and wine in condemnation and for judgment. This is also emphasized in the beautiful Cherubic Hymn which the choir sings while the priest prepares for the Great Entrance, "Let us who mystically represent the Cherubim and sing to the life creating Trinity, now lay aside all earthly that we may receive the King of All who comes upborne by the angelic hosts." We are reminded to lay aside all earthly cares, our agendas, plans, idols, and gods, in order to focus on the King of All who is Jesus Christ himself, who enters into the altar. This is again repeated a third time during the Liturgy in a somewhat similar fashion as we all say together the confession of faith just prior to receiving Holy Communion, "I believe O Lord and I confess that this is truly the most holy and precious body and blood ..." Again, since we are absent-minded creatures in this world we need to be constantly reminded of our calling to follow the Lord.

7

Peter's Confession of Faith (Mark 8:27-31)

When Thou shall come O righteous judge

To execute just judgment

Seated on thy throne of glory

A river of fire will draw all men amazed before thy judgment seat

The powers of heaven will stand beside thee

And in fear mankind will be judged according to the deeds that each
has done

Then spare us, O Christ, in Thy compassion

With faith we entreat Thee

Count us worthy of Thy blessings with those who are saved

(Stickhera for Vespers Sunday of the Last Judgment)

When reading the scriptures it is important that we read it as a complete whole from beginning to end. This is difficult because the liturgical calendar provides us with small portions of the scriptures that are taken from various chapters throughout the Bible. We cannot read an entire book of scripture during the Liturgy. Yet as was said before, it is important to become familiar with the entire Word of God. The more often we read and study the scriptures the more familiar we will become with the names, places, and events recorded in the Bible. Furthermore, the more familiar we become with the scriptures the more time we can devote ourselves to focusing on particular passages for study and reflection.

However, we always need to keep in mind the context of the particular reading. For example, today's reading from chapter eight is in the middle of the gospel of Mark. In other words, since Mark only has sixteen chapters, Peter's confession of faith on the road to Caeserea-Philipi appears exactly in the middle which means that it is the halfway part of the story. Usually a part of a story, such as the midpoint, is very important. Many plays and operas have important transition moments right in the middle of the performance. The same sentiment applies to the scriptures. The midway point is very important. Here in the middle of the gospel of Mark, Peter makes a public confession of faith.

The geographic setting for today's reading is the area called Caeserea-Philippi. Caesarea-Philippi was a Gentile city that was built by King Philip the son of Herod the Great. The city was named in honor of Augustus Caesar and King Philip, hence the combined name of Caeserea-Philippi which represents the power of Rome as well as the power of the Jewish people. The book of Acts also tells us that it was in Caeserea-Philippi where the Roman centurion Cornelius was converted by Peter (Acts 10).

This information is very important since it provides the context and background for today's lesson. As Jesus and his disciples were walking Jesus inquires of Peter, "Who do men say that I am." Peter answered, "You are the Christ." Jesus' question echoes other passages in scripture where the demons know Jesus' true identity while his disciples and friends do not such as we saw earlier in chapter one where the demon identified Jesus as the "Holy one of God" (Mark 1:24). Later in chapter four when Jesus and his disciples are on the sea of Galilee a storm arises. Jesus calms the storm and at the end his own disciples question, "Who the is this, that the wind and sea obey him?" (Mark 4:41).

Most of us have heard both the terms Christ and son of God. However, the title son of God was not unique to Jesus, the Roman emperors also used this title when referring to their power and authority over the empire. During the reign of Augustus Caesar, the emperor who reigned during the reign of Augustus Caesar people were encouraged to offer worship to the emperor as an act of public worship. The emperor was now considered to be the son of a god. There are archaeology findings that support the fact that one of Augustus' titles was "son of a god." Likewise, it was during this time when the Roman emperors demanded that temples be established in their honor and that the Roman citizens offer sacrifices in their name.

Therefore, in the middle of a Roman Gentile city, named after the great King Philip and Augustus Caesar, Peter confesses Jesus as the true Christ, the anointed one of God who is also the son of God. He makes this confession of faith disregarding the fact that during this same time it was the emperor himself who demanded the ultimate respect and honor. Peter's confession of faith in this location truly goes against every aspect of the Roman and temporal way of life. It is God alone who is due praise, worship, and hence honor. While Peter may seem to be very weak and perhaps a bit aloof, this public confession of faith is very important. Later, Paul will acknowledge Jesus as the Lord and savior to the Jews in the synagogues, but also to the Gentiles in all parts of the empire. Paul was not afraid to acknowledge Jesus as his Lord and savior. According to the scriptures, the true authority in this world is not the temporal governments or financial systems, not the businesses or politics, but Jesus himself. Hopefully we ca acknowledge Jesus as our Lord and savior in our day and age.

8

Jesus Predicts the End (Mark 10:32-45)

Behold the Bridegroom comes at midnight
And blessed is the servant whom he shall find watching
But unworthy is he whom he shall find heedless
Beware O my soul do not be wayed down in sleep
Lest you should be given over to death and shut out of the Kingdom
But rouse yourself crying: holy, holy, holy, art Thou O Lord
Through the prayer of the Theotokos have mercy on us!
(Troparion for Bridegroom Matins for Holy Week)

For the third and final time Jesus predicts his death. Two of his disciples, James and John the sons of Zebedee, argue about who is going to be the greatest in the kingdom. In chapter eight Jesus warns his disciples that he is going to Jerusalem where the Jewish leaders will mock and scourge him and put him to death (Mark 8:31-33).

Immediately following Jesus prediction of his death, two of his disciples, James and John the sons of Zebedee ask Jesus, "Teacher, we want you to do for us whatever we ask of you." And he said to them, "What do you want me to do for you?" And they said to him, "Grant us to sit, one at your right hand and one at your left, in your glory" (Mark 10:35-37).

It seems inconceivable, even comical, that these two brothers who have been with Jesus for a long time, who witnessed his miracles and heard his teachings, do not understand Jesus' teaching, even towards the end of the gospel. Twice before in the gospel, Jesus predicts his approaching death; his trial, suffering, and crucifixion. They saw Jesus rebuke Peter on the way to Caeserea-Philippi, and now these two brothers question Jesus' ministry. Rather, they are concerned about having the best seats in the kingdom, which really translates into they want atten-

31

tion and recognition for their ministry as disciples. They want earthly power, authority, and recognition, everything that goes against Jesus' own teaching and ministry. Jesus turns around and tells them, "but if shall not be so among you; but whoever would be great among you must be your servant, and whoever would be first among you must be slave of all. For the Son of man came not be served, and to give his life as a ransom for many" (Mark 10:43-45).

Jesus' indignation towards James and John is also developed as a theme in the gospel of John. In the thirteenth chapter of John, Jesus stoops down, takes off his tunic and begins to wash the feet of his disciples. At the end of the foot-washing scene Jesus tells his disciples, "You call me Teacher and Lord; and you are right, for so I am. If I then, your Lord and Teacher, have washed your feet, you also ought to wash one another's feet. For I have given you an example, that you should do as I have done to you" (John 13:12-15). Clearly both of these two passages focus our attention on humility and service. Not only does Jesus teach about serving one another by teaching, but he shows them by doing it himself. Jesus comes as a humble servant who comes and serves. In most English translations the word servant is used for the Greek word which means slave. In other words, Jesus is a slave who is bound to obey the will of the Father and who accepts the suffering and death on Golgotha. The Apostle Paul picks up this theme in his epistles and refers to himself as slave as well, when he refers to himself as Paul an apostle and a servant of God it really is Paul an apostle and slave of God. Paul does this through laying down his life for his communities, through visiting them, and comforting and consoling them in times of duress. Paul went through many trials, tribulations, torture, and imprisonment for his faith, he saw his life as being poured out as an offering for his communities. Paul's own life, in both word and deed, is seen in terms of Jesus' own life and ministry.

The term "slave" may seem pejorative in our contemporary society because we have a long history of racial slavery which was certainly terrible and ungodly. However, during the time of Jesus and Paul slavery was a regular part of the culture and society. Whenever the Roman army won a battle they obtained new slaves. Slaves were completely obedient to their masters and served them well. In many of Paul's epistles he refers to himself as "Paul, a servant of Jesus Christ" which actually translates as Paul, a slave of Jesus Christ (Romans 1:1 and Philippians 1:1). In the Roman empire a slave was bound to the house of the master and was considered property. If a slave tried to escape his master, the slave could be arrested and returned to the owner since the slave was considered to be material possession. The purpose of a household slave was to work on the property and take care of the needs of the family. Basically Jesus tells his disciples that there is no room for earthly or material recognition in this world or the world to come, only service of the neighbor.

This theme of service and humility is seen throughout the gospel as well as in the liturgical hymns of the Church. During Holy Week many Churches place a special icon in the Church called the icon of "Extreme Humility" which depicts Jesus on a cross and the bottom portion pictures his body in the tomb. In many ways today's gospel lesson prepares us for the period of Holy Week since throughout the entire Lenten season we follow Jesus to his suffering and his passion. Throughout Lent we heard passages from Mark that in a very brief way recall Jesus' entire ministry, the calling of his disciples, his ministry in the Galilee area, his preaching and teaching, and finally, his prediction of the end. We venerated a decorated cross in the middle of the Church as a reminder of where Jesus is headed, and likewise where we are headed. The cross is the symbol of our Christian faith.

These few weeks in the Church year are really powerful if we realize that it is a season for repentance and change. However, the real proof of our faith is not just living a life of repentance during Lent, but throughout the year. Or prayers, fasting, almsgiving, and scripture readings are in vain if we stop doing them after Lent. The gospel of Mark reminds us once again that we are supposed to hear Jesus call to obedience and faith as we heard as Jesus called Levi by asking, "Follow me." Are we going to follow Jesus wherever he leads us? Are we doing to drop our agendas and plans in order to put Jesus first in our lives? Are we going to live a life of humility and service, seeking to love and serve God with all of our mind, heart, soul, and strength?

Hopefully Lent will be a good time for us, a time to lay aside our earthly cares, wants, needs, and anxieties, becoming more dependant and faithful to Christ and the gospel. Perhaps this Lent will be a true Lenten Spring, a time when the Word of God grows and blossoms in our lives. A time for taking our first steps towards the Kingdom of Heaven.

APPENDIX

Patristic Texts on the Gospel of Mark

John Chrysostom (died 407)

John was born in Antioch in 347. Like Gregory, John had a classical education that included both rhetoric and philosophy. John studied under the direction of the great philosopher Libanius. When John returned to Antioch he befriended Bishop Meletius who baptized John and then ordained him to the diaconate. After baptism, Chrysostom entered the dessert for six years. He put himself under the care and guidance of Diodore of Tarsus, the famous Antiochene exegete. Diodore established a school for the learning and interpretation of scripture and was sought out as one of the greatest teachers of scripture in the Christian East. His students lived an austere lifestyle devoted to fasting and prayer with the remainder of time devoted to studying scripture.

Under the new bishop Flavian, John assisted in assisting the poor and needy, and even though he was a deacon, preached frequently in Church. In 398 John was appointed bishop in Constantinople where he found himself at the center of the Roman Empire. While in Constantinople John had different duties then when he was a priest yet he still continued to preach and teach as was his custom. As bishop, John's responsibilities were devoted the financial well being of the diocese as well as maintaining peace and concord among the clergy and local parish churches. John was the chief pastor in the capital city and therefore had much greater responsibilities then when he was a priest. However, while his obligations took him to various places and locations John always cared for his community and preached sermons about repentance, love, forgiveness, and salvation.

Throughout his ecclesiastical career at Antioch and Constantinople John devoted himself to preaching the gospel and ministering to the church of Christ. Chrysostom encountered a lot of resistance to the truth from the rich upper class of society and the political leaders. However, John's only weapon was gospel of Christ and he used it whenever he had the opportunity. The vast number of his sermons and homilies that survive testify to this fact. John certainly earned the name "golden mouth" and priests and pastors still look to him as an example of as a true pastor of Christ's flock. St. John is commemorated on November 13 and on January 30 together with, Basil the Great and Gregory the Theologian.

For Further Reading:

St. John Chrysostom *On Marriage and Family* translated by Catherine P. Roth and David Anderson (Crestwood, NY: St. Vladimir's Seminary Press, 1986).

----------------------------*On Wealth and Poverty* translated by Catherine P. Roth (Crestwood, NY: St. Vladimir's Seminary Press, 1984).

---------------------------*Six Books on the Priesthood* translated by Graham Neville (Crestwood, NY: St Vladimir's Seminary Press, 1984).

-----------------------------*Baptismal Instructions* translated Paul W. Harkins (Mahwah, NJ: Paulist Press, 1963).

------------------------------*On The Cult of the Saints* translated Wendy Mayer with Browen Neil (Crestwood, NY: St. Vladimir's Seminary Press, 2006).

Wendy Mayer and Pauline Allen *John Chrysostom* (NY: Routledge, 2000).

J.N.D Kelly *Golden Mouth: The Story of John Chrysostom: Asectic, Preacher, Bishop* (Grand Rapids, MI: Baker Books, 1995).

Sermon on Matthew 14:13

"Now when Jesus had gone forth into the coasts of Caesarea Philippi, He asked His disciples, saying, Whom do men say that I the Son of Man am?"

Wherefore has he mentioned the founder of the city? Because there was another besides, Cæsarea Stratonis. But not in that, but in this does He ask them, leading them far away from the Jews, so that being freed from all alarm, they might speak with boldness all that was in their mind.

And wherefore did He not ask them at once their own opinion, but that of the people? In order that when they had told the people's opinion, and then were asked, "But whom say ye that I am?" by the manner of His inquiry they might be led up to a sublimer notion, and not fall into the same low view as the multitude. Accordingly He asks them not at all in the beginning of His preaching, but when He had done many miracles, and had discoursed with them of many and high doctrines, and had afforded so many clear proofs of His Godhead, and of His unanimity with the Father, then He puts this question to them.

And He said not, "Whom say the Scribes and Pharisees that I am?" often as these had come unto Him, and discoursed with Him; but, "Whom do men say that I am?" inquiring after the judgment of the people, as unbiassed. For though it was far meaner than it should be, yet was it free from malice, but the other was teeming with much wickedness.

And signifying how earnestly He desires His Economyto be confessed, He says, "The Son of Man;" thereby denoting His Godhead, which He does also in many other places. For He says, "No man has ascended up to Heaven, but the Son of Man, which is in Heaven." John 3:13 And again, "But when you shall see the Son of Man ascend up, where He was before." John 6:62

Then, since they said, "Some John the Baptist, some Elias, some Jeremias, or one of the prophets," Matthew 16:14 and set forth their mistaken opinion, He next added, "But whom say ye that I am?" Matthew 16:15 calling them on by His second inquiry to entertain some higher imagination concerning Him, and indicating that their former judgment falls exceedingly short of His dignity. Wherefore He seeks for another judgment from themselves, and puts a second question, that they might not fall in with the multitude, who, because they saw His miracles greater than human, accounted Him a man indeed, but one that had appeared after a resurrection, as Herod also said. Matthew 14:2 But He, to lead them away from this notion, says, "But whom say ye that I am?" that is, "ye that are with me always, and see me working miracles, and have yourselves done many mighty works by me."

2. What then says the mouth of the apostles, Peter, the ever fervent, the leader of the apostolic choir? When all are asked, he answers. And whereas when He asked the opinion of the people, all replied to the question; when He asked their own, Peter springs forward, and anticipates them, and says, "You are the Christ, the Son of the living God." Matthew 16:16

What then says Christ? "Blessed are you, Simon Barjona, for flesh and blood has not revealed it unto you." Matthew 16:17

Yet surely unless he had rightly confessed Him, as begotten of the very Father Himself, this were no work of revelation; had he accounted our Lord to be one of the many, his saying was not worthy of a blessing. Since before this also they said, "Truly He is Son of God," Matthew 14:33 those, I mean, who were in the vessel after the tempest, which they saw, and were not blessed, although of course they spoke truly. For they confessed not such a Sonship as Peter, but accounted Him to be truly Son as one of the many, and though peculiarly so beyond the many, yet not of the same substance.

And Nathanael too said, "Rabbi, You are the Son of God, You are the King of Israel;" John 1:49 and so far from being blessed, he is even reproved by Him, as having said what was far short of the truth. He replied at least, "Because I said unto you, I saw you under the fig-tree, do you believe? you shall see greater things than these." John 1:50

Why then is this man blessed? Because he acknowledged Him very Son. Wherefore you see, that while in those former instances He had said no such thing, in this case He also signifies who had revealed it. That is, lest his words might seem to the many (because he was an earnest lover of Christ) to be words of friendship and flattery, and of a disposition to show favor to Him, he brings forward the person who had made them ringin his soul; to inform you that Peter indeed spoke, but the Father suggested, and that you might believe the saying to be no longer a human opinion, but a divine doctrine.

And wherefore does He not Himself declare it, nor say, "I am the Christ," but by His question establish this, bringing them in to confess it? Because so to do was both more suitable to Him, yea necessary at that time, and it drew them on the more to the belief of the things that were said.

Do you see how the Father reveals the Son, how the Son the Father? For "neither knows any man the Father," says He, "save the Son, and he to whomsoever the Son will reveal Him." It cannot therefore be that one should learn the Son of any other than of the Father; neither that one should learn the Father of any other than of the Son. So that even hereby, their sameness of honor and of substance is manifest.

3. What then says Christ? "You are Simon, the son of Jonas; you shall be called Cephas." "Thus since you have proclaimed my Father, I too name him that begat you;" all but saying, "As you are son of Jonas, even so am I of my Father." Else it were superfluous to say, "You are Son of Jonas;" but since he had said, "Son of God," to point out that He is so Son of God, as the other son of Jonas, of the same substance with Him that begat Him, therefore He added this, "And I say unto you, You are Peter, and upon this rock will I build my Church;" Matthew 16:18 that is, on the faith of his confession. Hereby He signifies that many were now on the point of believing, and raises his spirit, and makes him a shepherd. "And the gates of hellshall not prevail against it." "And if not against it, much more not against me. So be not troubled because you are shortly to hear that I shall be betrayed and crucified."

Then He mentions also another honor. "And I alsowill give you the keys of the heavens." But what is this, "And I also will give you?" "As the Father has given you to know me, so will I also give you."

And He said not, "I will entreat the Father" (although the manifestation of His authority was great, and the largeness of the gift unspeakable), but, "I will give you." What dost Thou give? tell me. "The keys of the heavens, that whatsoever you shall bind on earth, shall be bound in Heaven, and whatsoever you shall loose on earth, shall be loosed in Heaven." How then is it not "His to give to sit on His right hand, and on His left," Matthew 20:23 when He says, "I will give you"?

Do you see how He, His own self, leads Peter on to high thoughts of Him, and reveals Himself, and implies that He is Son of God by these two promises? For those things which are peculiar to God alone, (both to absolve sins, and to make the church in capable of overthrow in such assailing waves, and to exhibit a man that is a fisher more solid than any rock, while all the world is at war with him), these He promises Himself to give; as the Father, speaking to Jeremiah, said, He would make him as "a brazen pillar, and as a wall;" but him to one nation only, this man in every part of the world.

I would fain inquire then of those who desire to lessen the dignity of the Son, which manner of gifts were greater, those which the Father gave to Peter, or those which the Son gave him? For the Father gave to Peter the revelation of the Son; but the Son gave him to sow that of the Father and that of Himself in every part of the world; and to a mortal man He entrusted the authority over all things in Heaven, giving him the keys; who extended the church to every part of the world, and declared it to be stronger than heaven. "For heaven and earth shall pass away, but my word shall not pass away." Matthew 24:35 How then is He less, who has given such gifts, has effected such things?

And these things I say, not dividing the works of Father and Son ("for all things are made by Him, and without Him was nothing made which was made"):but bridling the shameless tongue of them that dare so to speak.

But see, throughout all, His authority: "I say unto you, You are Peter; I will build the Church; I will give you the keys of Heaven."

4. And then, when He had so said, "He charged them that they should tell no man that He was the Christ." Matthew 16:20

And why did He charge them? That when the things which offend are taken out of the way, and the cross is accomplished, and the rest of His sufferings fulfilled, and when there is nothing any more to interrupt and disturb the faith of the people in Him, the right opinion concerning Him may be engraven pure and immovable in the mind of the hearers. For, in truth, His power had not yet clearly shone forth. Accordingly it was His will then to be preached by them, when both the plain truth of the facts, and the power of His deeds were pleading in support of the assertions of the apostles. For it was by no means the same thing to see Him in Palestine, now working miracles, and now insulted and persecuted (and especially when the very cross was presently to follow the miracles that were happening); and to behold him everywhere in the world, adored and believed, and no more suffering anything, such as He had suffered.

Therefore He bids them "tell no man." For that which has been once rooted and then plucked up, would hardly, if planted, again be retained among the many; but that which, once fixed, has remained immovable, and has suffered injury from no quarter, easily mounts up, and advances to a greater growth.

And if they who had enjoyed the benefit of many miracles, and had had part in so many unutterable mysteries, were offended by the mere hearing of it; or rather not these only, but even the leaderof them all, Peter; consider what it was likely the common sort should feel, being first told that He is the Son of God, then seeing Him even crucified and spit upon, and that without knowledge of the secret of those mysteries, or participation in the gift of the Holy Ghost. For if to His disciples He said, "I have many things to say unto you, but ye cannot bear them now;" John 16:12 much more would the rest of the people have utterly failed, had the chiefest of these mysteries been revealed to them before the proper time. Accordingly He forbids them to tell.

And to instruct you how great a thing it was, their afterwards learning His doctrine complete, when the things that offend had passed by; learn it from this same leader of theirs. For this very Peter, he who after so many miracles proved so weak as even to deny Him, and to be in fear of a mean damsel; after the cross had come forth, and he had received the certain proofs of the resurrection, and there was nothing more to offend and trouble him, retained the teaching of the Spirit so immovable, that more vehemently than a lion he sprang upon the people of the Jews, for all the dangers and innumerable deaths which were threatened.

With reason then did He bid them not tell the many before the crucifixion, since not even to them that were to teach did He venture to commit all before the crucifixion. "For I have many things to say unto you," says He, "but ye cannot bear them now."

And of the things too that He did say, they do not understand many, which He did not make plain before the crucifixion. At least when He was risen from the dead, then and not before they knew some of His sayings.

5. "From that time forth began He to show unto them that He must suffer. Matthew 16:21 From that time." What time? When He had fixed the doctrine in them; when He had brought in the beginning of the Gentiles.

But not even so did they understand what He said. "For the saying," it is said, "was hid from them;" Luke 18:34 and they were as in a kind of perplexity, not knowing that He must rise again. Therefore He rather dwells on the difficulties, and enlarges His discourse, that He may open their mind, and they may understand what it can be that He speaks of.

"But they understood not, but the saying was hid from them, and they feared to ask this;" Luke 9:45 not whether He should die, but how, and in what manner, and what this mystery could be. For they did not even know what was this same rising again, and supposed it much better not to die. Therefore, the rest being troubled and in perplexity, Peter again, in his ardor, alone ventures to discourse of these things; and not even he openly, but when he had taken Him apart; that is, having separated himself from the rest of the disciples; and he says, "Be it far from You, Lord, this shall not be unto You." What ever is this? He that obtained a revelation, he that was blessed, has he so soon fallen away, and suffered overthrow, so as to fear His passion? And what marvel, that one who had not on these points received any revelation, should have that feeling? Yea, to inform you that not of himself did he speak those other things either, see in these matters that were not revealed to him how he is confounded and overthrown, and being told ten thousand times, knows not what the saying can mean.

For that He is Son of God he had learned, but what the mystery of the cross and of the resurrection might be, was not yet manifest to him: for "the saying," it is said, "was hid from them."

Do you see that with just cause He bade them not declare it to the rest? For if it so confounded them, who must needs be made aware of it, what would not all others have felt?

6. He however, to signify that He is far from coming to the passion against His will, both rebuked Peter, and called him Satan.

Let them hear, as many as are ashamed of the suffering of the cross of Christ. For if the chief apostle, even before he had learned all distinctly, was called Satan for feeling this, what excuse can they have, who after so abundant proof deny His economy? I say, when he who had been so blessed, who made such a confession, has such words addressed to him; consider what they will suffer, who after all this deny the mystery of the cross.

And He said not, "Satan spoke by you," but, "Get behind me, Satan." Matthew 16:23 For indeed it was a desire of the adversary that Christ should not suffer. Therefore with such great severity did He rebuke him, as knowing that both he and the rest are especially afraid of this, and will not easily receive it.

Therefore He also reveals the thoughts of his mind, saying, "Thou savorestnot the things that be of God, but those that be of men."

But what means, "Thou savorestnot the things that be of God, but those that be of men"? Peter examining the matter by human and earthly reasoning, accounted it disgraceful to Him and an unmeet thing. Touching him therefore sharply, He says, "My passion is not an unmeet thing, but you give this sentence with a carnal mind; whereas if you had hearkened to my sayings in a godly manner, disengaging yourself from your carnal understanding, you would know that this of all things most becomes me. For thou indeed supposest that to suffer is unworthy of me; but I say unto you, that for me not to suffer is of the devil's mind;" by the contrary statements repressing his alarm.

Thus as John, accounting it unworthy of Christ to be baptized by him, was persuaded of Christ to baptize Him, He saying, "Thus it becomes us," Matthew 3:15 and this same Peter too, forbidding Him to wash his feet, by the words, "You have no part with me, unless I wash your feet;" John 13:8 even so here too He restrained him by the mention of the opposite, and by the severity of the reproof repressed his fear of suffering.

7. Let no man therefore be ashamed of the honored symbols of our salvation, and of the chiefest of all good things, whereby we even live, and whereby we are; but as a crown, so let us bear about the cross of Christ. Yea, for by it all things are wrought, that are wrought among us. Whether one is to be new-born, the cross is there; or to be nourished with that mystical food, or to be ordained, or to do anything else, everywhere our symbol of victory is present. Therefore both on house,

and walls, and windows, and upon our forehead, and upon our mind, we inscribe it with much care.

For of the salvation wrought for us, and of our common freedom, and of the goodness of our Lord, this is the sign. "For as a sheep was He led to the slaughter." Isaiah 53:7 When therefore you sign yourself, think of the purpose of the cross, and quench anger, and all the other passions. When you sign yourself, fill your forehead with all courage, make your soul free. And ye know assuredly what are the things that give freedom. Wherefore also Paul leading us there, I mean unto the freedom that beseems us, did on this wise lead us unto it, having reminded us of the cross and blood of our Lord. "For you are bought," says he, "with a price; be not ye the servants of men." Consider, says he, the price that has been paid for you, and you will be a slave to no man; by the price meaning the cross.

Since not merely by the fingers ought one to engrave it, but before this by the purpose of the heart with much faith. And if in this way you have marked it on your face, none of the unclean spirits will be able to stand near you, seeing the blade whereby he received his wound, seeing the sword which gave him his mortal stroke. For if we, on seeing the places in which the criminals are beheaded, shudder; think what the devil must endure, seeing the weapon, whereby Christ put an end to all his power, and cut off the head of the dragon.

Be not ashamed then of so great a blessing, lest Christ be ashamed of you, when He comes with His glory, and the sign appears before Him, shining beyond the very sunbeam. For indeed the cross comes then, uttering a voice by its appearance, and pleading with the whole world for our Lord, and signifying that no part has failed of what pertained to Him.

This sign, both in the days of our forefathers and now, has opened doors that were shut up;this has quenched poisonous drugs; this has taken away the power of hemlock; this has healed bites of venomous beasts. For if it opened the gates of hell, and threw wide the archways of Heaven, and made a new entrance into Paradise, and cut away the nerves of the devil; what marvel, if it prevailed over poisonous drugs, and venomous beasts, and all other such things.

This therefore do thou engrave upon your mind, and embrace the salvation of our souls. For this cross saved and converted the world, drove away error, brought back truth, made earth Heaven, fashioned men into angels. Because of this, the devils are no longer terrible, but contemptible; neither is death, death, but a sleep; because of this, all that wars against us is cast to the ground, and trodden under foot.

If any one therefore say to you, Do you worship the crucified? say, with your voice all joy, and your countenance gladdened, "I do both worship Him, and will never cease to worship." And if he laugh, weep for him, because he is mad. Thank the Lord, that He has bestowed on us such benefits, as one cannot so much as learn without His revelation from above. Why, this is the very reason of his laughing, that "the natural man receives not the things of the Spirit."
1 Corinthians 2:14 Since our children too feel this, when they see any of the great and marvellous things; and if thou bring a child into the mysteries, he will laugh. Now the heathen are like these children; or rather they are more imperfect even than these; wherefore also they are more wretched, in that not in an immature age, but when full grown, they have the feelings of babes; wherefore neither are they worthy of indulgence.

But let us with a clear voice, shouting both loud and high, cry out and say (and should all the heathen be present, so much the more confidently), that the cross is our glory, and the sum of all our blessings, and our confidence, and all our crown. I would that also with Paul I were able to say, "By which the world is crucified unto me, and I unto the world;" Galatians 6:14 but I cannot, restrained as I am by various passions.

8. Wherefore I admonish both you, and surely before you myself, to be crucified to the world, and to have nothing in common with the earth, but to set your love on your country above, and the glory and the good things that come from it. For indeed we are soldiers of a heavenly King, and are clad with spiritual arms. Why then take we upon ourselves the life of traders, and mountebanks, nay rather of worms? For where the King is, there should also the soldier be. Yea, we are become soldiers, not of them that are far off, but of them that are near. For the earthly king indeed would not endure that all should be in the royal courts, and at his own side, but the King of the Heavens wills all to be near His royal throne.

And how, one may say, is it possible for us, being here, to stand by that throne? Because Paul too being on earth was where the seraphim, where the cherubim are; and nearer to Christ, than these the body guards to the king. For these turn about their faces in many directions, but him nothing beguiled nor distracted, but he kept his whole mind intent upon the king. So that if we would, this is possible to us also.

For were He distant from us in place, you might well doubt, but if He is present everywhere, to him that strives and is in earnest He is near. Wherefore also the prophet said, "I will fear no evil, for You are with me;" and God Himself again, "I am a God nigh at hand, and not a God afar off." Then as our sins separate us from Him, so do our righteousnesses draw us nigh unto Him. "For while you are yet speaking," it is said, "I will say, Here I am." What father would ever be thus obedient to his offspring? What mother is there, so ready, and continually standing, if haply her children call her? There is not one, no father, no mother: but God stands continually waiting, if any of his servants should perchance call Him; and never, when we have called as we ought, has He refused to hear. Therefore He says, "While you are yet speaking," I do not wait for you to finish, and I straightway hearken.

9. Let us call Him therefore, as it is His will to be called. But what is this His will? "Loose," says He, "every band of iniquity, unloose the twisted knots of oppressive covenants, tear in pieces every unjust contract. Break your bread to the hungry, and bring in the poor that are cast out to your house. If you see one naked, cover him, and them that belong to your seed you shall not overlook. Then shall your light break forth in the morning, and thine healings shall spring forth speedily, and your righteousness shall go before you, and the glory of the Lord shall cover you. Then you shall call upon me, and I will give ear unto you; while you are yet speaking, I will say, Lo! here I am."

And who is able to do all this? it may be asked. Nay, who is unable, I pray you? For which is difficult of the things I have mentioned? Which is laborious? Which not easy?

Why, so entirely are they not possible only, but even easy, that many have actually overshot the measure of those sayings, not only tearing in pieces unjust contracts, but even stripping themselves of all their goods; making the poor welcome not to roof and table, but even to the sweat of their body, and laboring in order to maintain them; doing good not to kinsmen only, but even to enemies.

But what is there at all even hard in these sayings? For neither did He say, "Pass over the mountain, go across the sea, dig through so many acres of land, abide without food, wrap yourself in sackcloth;" but, "Impart to the poor, impart of your bread, cancel the contracts unjustly made."

What is more easy than this? tell me. But even if thou account it difficult, look, I pray you, at the rewards also, and it shall be easy to you.

For much as our emperors at the horse races heap together before the combatants crowns, and prizes, and garments, even so Christ also sets His rewards in the midst of His course, holding them out by the prophet's words, as it were by many hands. And the emperors, although they be ten thousand times emperors, yet as being men, and the wealth which they have in a course of spending, and their munificence of exhaustion, are ambitious of making the little appear much; wherefore also they commit each thing severally into the hand of the several attendants, and so bring it forward. But our King contrariwise, having heaped all together (because He is very rich, and does nothing for display), He so brings it forward, and what He so reaches out is indefinitely great, and will need many hands to hold it. And to make you aware of this, examine each particular of it carefully.

"Then," says He, "shall your light break forth in the morning." Doth not this gift appear to you as some one thing? But it is not one; nay, for it has many things in it, both prizes, and crowns, and other rewards. And, if you are minded, let us take it to pieces and show all its wealth, as it shall be possible for us to show it; only do not ye grow weary.

And first, let us learn the meaning of "It shall break forth." For He said not at all, "shall appear," but "shall break forth;" declaring to us its quickness and plentifulness, and how exceedingly He desires our salvation, and how the good things themselves travail to come forth, and press on; and that which would check their unspeakable force shall be nought; by all which He indicates their plentifulness, and the infinity of His abundance. But what is "the morning." It means, "not after being in life's temptations, neither after our evils have come upon us;" nay, it is quite beforehand with them. For as in our fruits, we call that early, which has shown itself before its season; so also here again, declaring its rapidity, he has spoken in this way, much as above He said, "Whilst you are yet speaking, I will say, Lo! here I am."

But of what manner of light is He speaking, and what can this light be? Not this, that is sensible; but another far better, which shows us Heaven, the angels, the archangels, the cherubim, the seraphim, the thrones, the dominions, the principalities, the powers, the whole host, the royal palaces, the tabernacles. For should you be counted worthy of this light, you shall both see these, and be delivered from hell, and from the venomous worm, and from the gnashing of teeth, and from the bonds that cannot be broken, and from the anguish and the affliction, from the darkness that has no light, and from being cut asunder, and from the river of fire, and from the curse, and from the abodes of sorrow; and you shall depart, "where sorrow and woe are fled away," Isaiah 35:10 where great is the joy, and the peace, and the love, and the pleasure, and the mirth; where is life eternal, and unspeakable glory, and inexpressible beauty; where are eternal tabernacles, and the untold glory of the King, and those good things, "which eye has not seen, nor ear heard, neither have entered into the heart of man;" 1 Corinthians 2:9 where is the spiritual bridechamber, and the apartments of the heavens, and the virgins that bear the bright lamps, and they who have the marriage garment; where many are the possessions of our Lord, and the storehouses of the King.

Do you see how great the rewards, and how many He has set forth by one expression, and how He brought all together?

So also by unfolding each of the expressions that follow, we shall find our abundance great, and the ocean immense. Shall we then still delay, I beg you; and be backward to show mercy on them that are in need? Nay, I entreat, but though we must throw away all, be cast into the fire, venture against the sword, leap upon daggers, suffer what you will; let us bear all easily, that we may obtain the garment of the kingdom of Heaven, and that untold glory; which may we all attain, by the grace and love towards man of our Lord Jesus Christ, to whom be glory and might, world without end. Amen.

Augustine of Hippo (died 430)

Augustine is one of the most prolific of the Church Fathers. His collected works including his theological orations, sermons, letters, and pastoral reflections take up several bookshelves in a library. He is remembered not only as a bishop and administrator of the Church but a true pastor, caring for his flock in Hippo and preaching the gospel of the Lord. There are numerous biographies about his life as well as his famous autobiography called *The Confessions* where he speaks about the spiritual life in general and his own personal journey to Christianity as well.

Augustine was born in north Africa to Patricius and Monica. His father Patricius was a local government official who was a pagan and Monica was a devout Christian who prayed for her son Augustine's conversion to the Christian faith. His father sent him to the north African city of Carthage where he studied law and rhetoric. He eventually fell into the heretical teachings of Manichesim which was taught by Mani. Manichesim was based on a gnostic teaching of duality that the flesh was bad and the spirit is good. Manicheism was very popular during this time and many priests and bishops had to fight against these false teachings. Eventually Augustine traveled to Rome where he met Ambrose, Bishop of Milan. Through many conversations with Ambrose, Augustine realized his errors and accepted to be baptized into the Christian faith. He was baptized sometime in great Lent in 387.

In 396, Augustine became the bishop of Hippo, a small city in North Africa where he served until his death in 438. Augustine lived an austere lifestyle choosing to live in a monastic community rather in a special bishop's residence. The monastic community revolved around regular hours of prayer, community work, and time for reading and contemplation. Eventually Augustine wrote down their way of life in the Monastic Rules which are still used today by the Augustinian Brothers who follow the Rule of St. Augustine in the Catholic Church.

As was stated previously, Augustine was a prolific orator and theologian. He delivered many sermons and theological orations in his cathedral. Like Leo, Augustine had a pastoral heart and his sermons reflect his devotion to the scriptures. Unfortunately many scholars have focused their attention more on his theological writings which are many, yet his commentaries on the scriptures are worth more research and study. His homilies on Matthew and on the other gospels show a connection between the gospels and daily life, looking to Jesus Christ as the supreme example of love.

For Further Reading:

Augustine of Hippo *Confessions* Garry Wills (ed.) (NY: Penguin, 2006)

----------------------*The Monastic Rules* (NY: New City Press, 2004)

Brown, Peter *Augustine of Hippo Rev. Ed.* (Berkeley, The University of California Press, 2000)

O'Donnell, James J. *Augustine: A New Biography* (New York, Harper Perennial, 2005)

Wills, Garry *Saint Augustine* (New York, Penguin, 1999).

A Sermon n Matthew 14:25

Again on Matt. xiv. 25—: Of the Lord walking on the waves of the sea, and of Peter tottering.

1. The Gospel which has just been read touching the Lord Christ, who walked on the waters of the sea; and the Apostle Peter, who as he was walking, tottered through fear, and sinking in distrust, rose again by confession, gives us to understand that the sea is the present world, and the Apostle Peter the type of the One Church. For Peter in the order of Apostles first, and in the love of Christ most forward, answers oftentimes alone for all the rest. Again, when the Lord Jesus Christ asked, whom men said that He was, and when the disciples gave the various opinions of men, and the Lord asked again and said, "But whom say ye that I am?" Peter answered, "You are the Christ, the Son of the living God." One for many gave the answer, Unity in many. Then said the Lord to Him, "Blessed are you, Simon Barjonas: for flesh and blood has not revealed it unto you, but My Father which is in heaven." Then He added, "and I say unto you." As if He had said, "Because you have said unto Me, 'You are the Christ the Son of the living God;' I also say unto you, 'You are Peter.'" For before he was called Simon. Now this name of Peter was given him by the Lord, and that in a figure, that he should signify the Church. For seeing that Christ is the rock (Petra), Peter is the Christian people. For the rock (Petra) is the original name. Therefore Peter is so called from the rock; not the rock from Peter; as Christ is not called Christ from the Christian, but the Christian from Christ. "Therefore," he says, "You are Peter; and upon this Rock" which you have confessed, upon this Rock which you have acknowledged, saying, "You are the Christ, the Son of the living God, will I build My Church;" that is upon Myself, the Son of the living God, "will I build My Church." I will build you upon Myself, not Myself upon you.

2. For men who wished to be built upon men, said, "I am of Paul; and I of Apollos; and I of Cephas," who is Peter. But others who did not wish to be built upon Peter, but upon the Rock, said, "But I am of Christ." And when the Apostle Paul ascertained that he was chosen, and Christ despised, he said, "Is Christ divided? was Paul crucified for you? Or were ye baptized in the name of Paul?" And, as not in the name of Paul, so neither in the name of Peter; but in the name of Christ: that Peter might be built upon the Rock, not the Rock upon Peter.

3. This same Peter therefore who had been by the Rock pronounced "blessed," bearing the figure of the Church, holding the chief place in the Apostleship, a

very little while after that he had heard that he was "blessed," a very little while after that he had heard that he was "Peter," a very little while after that he had heard that he was to be "built upon the Rock," displeased the Lord when He had heard of His future Passion, for He had foretold His disciples that it was soon to be. He feared lest he should by death, lose Him whom he had confessed as the fountain of life. He was troubled, and said, "Be it far from You, Lord: this shall not be to You." Spare Yourself, O God, I am not willing that You should die. Peter said to Christ, I am not willing that You should die; but Christ far better said, I am willing to die for you. And then He forthwith rebuked him, whom He had a little before commended; and calls him Satan, whom he had pronounced "blessed." "Get behind Me, Satan," he says, "you are an offence unto Me: for you savour not the things that be of God, but those that be of men." What would He have us do in our present state, who thus finds fault because we are men? Would you know what He would have us do? Give ear to the Psalm; "I have said, You are gods, and you are all the children of the Most High." But by savouring the things of men; "you shall die like men." The very same Peter a little while before blessed, afterwards Satan, in one moment, within a few words! Thou wonderest at the difference of the names, mark the difference of the reasons of them. Why do you wonder that he who was a little before blessed, is afterwards Satan? Mark the reason wherefore he is blessed. "Because flesh and blood has not revealed it unto you, but My Father which is in heaven." Therefore blessed, because flesh and blood has not revealed it unto you. For if flesh and blood revealed this to you, it were of your own; but because flesh and blood has not revealed it unto you, but My Father which is in heaven, it is of Mine, not of your own. Why of Mine? "Because all things that the Father has are Mine." So then you have heard the cause, why he is "blessed," and why he is "Peter." But why was he that which we shudder at, and are loth to repeat, why, but because it was of your own? "For you savour not the things which be of God, but those that be of men."

4. Let us, looking at ourselves in this member of the Church, distinguish what is of God, and what of ourselves. For then we shall not totter, then shall we be founded on the Rock, shall be fixed and firm against the winds, and storms, and streams, the temptations, I mean, of this present world. Yet see this Peter, who was then our figure; now he trusts, and now he totters; now he confesses the Undying, and now he fears lest He should die. Wherefore? because the Church of Christ has both strong and weak ones; and cannot be without either strong or weak; whence the Apostle Paul says, "Now we that are strong ought to bear the infirmities of the weak." In that Peter said, "You are the Christ, the Son of the living God," he represents the strong: but in that he totters, and would not that

Christ should suffer, in fearing death for Him, and not acknowledging the Life, he represents the weak ones of the Church. In that one Apostle then, that is, Peter, in the order of Apostles first and chiefest, in whom the Church was figured, both sorts were to be represented, that is, both the strong and weak; because the Church does not exist without them both.

5. And hence also is that which was just now read, "Lord, if it be Thou, bid me come unto You on the water." For I cannot do this in myself, but in You. He acknowledged what he had of himself, and what of Him, by whose will he believed that he could do that, which no human weakness could do. Therefore, "if it be Thou, bid me;" because when you bid, it will be done. What I cannot do by taking it upon myself, You can do by bidding me. And the Lord said "Come." And without any doubting, at the word of Him who bade him, at the presence of Him who sustained, at the presence of Him who guided him, without any delay, Peter leaped down into the water, and began to walk. He was able to do what the Lord was doing, not in himself, but in the Lord. "For you were sometimes darkness, but now are you light in the Lord." What no one can do in Paul, no one in Peter, no one in any other of the Apostles, this can he do in the Lord. Therefore well said Paul by a wholesome despising of himself, and commending of Him; "Was Paul crucified for you, or were ye baptized in the name of Paul?" So then, you are not *in* me, but together *with* me; not under me, but under Him.

6. Therefore Peter walked on the water by the bidding of the Lord, knowing that he could not have this power of himself. By faith he had strength to do what human weakness could not do. These are the strong ones of the Church. Mark this, hear, understand, and act accordingly. For we must not deal with the strong on any other principle than this, that so they should become weak; but thus we must deal with the weak, that they may become strong. But the presuming on their own strength keeps many back from strength. No one will have strength from God, but he who feels himself weak of himself. "God sets apart a spontaneous rain for His inheritance." Why do you, who know what I was about to say, anticipate me? Let your quickness be moderated, that the slowness of the rest may follow. This I said, and I say it again; hear it, receive it, and act on this principle. No one is made strong by God, but he who feels himself weak of his own self. And therefore a "spontaneous rain," as the Psalm says, "spontaneous;" not of our deserts, but "spontaneous." "A spontaneous rain" therefore "God sets apart for his inheritance;" for "it was weak; but You have perfected it." Because Thou "hast set apart for it a spontaneous rain," not looking to men's deserts, but to Your own grace and mercy. This inheritance then was weakened, and acknowledged its own

weakness in itself, that it might be strong in You. It would not be strengthened, if it were not weak, that by You it might be "perfected" in You.

7. See Paul a small portion of this inheritance, see him in weakness, who said, "I am not meet to be called an Apostle, because I persecuted the Church of God." Why then are you an Apostle? "By the grace of God I am what I am. I am not meet, but by the grace of God I am what I am." Paul was "weak," but You have "perfected" him. But now because by "the grace of God he is what he is," look what follows; "And His grace in me was not in vain, but I laboured more abundantly than they all." Take heed lest you lose by presumption what you have attained through weakness. This is well, very well; that "I am not meet to be called an Apostle. By His grace I am what I am, and His grace in me was not in vain:" all most excellent. But, "I laboured more abundantly than they all;" you have begun, it would seem, to ascribe to yourself what a little before you had given to God. Attend and follow on; "Yet not I, but the grace of God with me." Well! you weak one; you shall be exalted in exceeding strength, seeing you are not unthankful. You are the very same Paul, little in yourself; and great in the Lord. You are he who thrice beseeched the Lord, that "the thorn of the flesh, the messenger of Satan, by whom you were buffeted, might be taken away from you." And what was said to you? what did you hear when you made this petition? "My grace is sufficient for you: for My strength is made perfect in weakness." For he was "weak," but Thou "perfected" him.

8. So Peter also said, "Bid me come unto You on the water." I who dare this am but a man, but it is no man whom I beseech. Let the God-man bid, that man may be able to do what man cannot do. "Come," said He. And He went down, and began to walk on the water; and Peter was able, because the Rock had bidden him. Lo, what Peter was in the Lord; what was he in himself? "When he saw the wind boisterous, he was afraid; and beginning to sink, he cried out, Lord, I perish, save me." When he looked for strength from the Lord, he had strength from the Lord; as a man he tottered, but he returned to the Lord. "If I said, my foot has slipped" (they are the words of a Psalm, the notes of a holy song; and if we acknowledge them they are our words too; yea, if we will, they are ours also). "If I said my foot has slipped." How slipped, except because it was my own. And what follows? "Your mercy, Lord, helped me." Not my own strength, but Your mercy. For will God forsake him as he totters, whom He heard when calling upon Him? Where then is that, "Who has called upon God, and has been forsaken by Him?" where again is that, "Whosoever shall call on the Name of the Lord, shall be delivered." Immediately reaching forth the help of His right hand, He lifted him

up as he was sinking, and rebuked his distrust; "O you of little faith, wherefore did you doubt?" Once you trusted in Me, have you now doubted of Me?

9. Well, brethren, my sermon must be ended. Consider the world to be the sea; the wind is boisterous, and there is a mighty tempest. Each man's peculiar lust is his tempest. Thou dost love God; you walk upon the sea, and under your feet is the swelling of the world. Thou dost love the world, it will swallow you up. It skills only how to devour its lovers, not to carry them. But when your heart is tossed about by lust, in order that you may get the better of your lust, call upon the Divinity of Christ. Think ye that the wind is then contrary, when there is this life's adversity? For so when there are wars, when there is tumult, when there is famine, when there is pestilence, when even to every individual man his private calamity arrives, then the wind is thought to be contrary, then it is thought that God must be called upon. But when the world wears her smile of temporal happiness, it is as if there were no contrary wind. But do not ask upon this matter the tranquil state of the times: ask only your own lust. See if there be tranquillity within you: see if there be no inner wind which overturns you; see to this. There needs great virtue to struggle with happiness, lest this very happiness allure, corrupt, and overthrow you. There needs, I say, great virtue to struggle with happiness, and great happiness not to be overcome by happiness. Learn then to tread upon the world; remember to trust in Christ. And "if your foot have slipped;" if you totter, if some things there are which you can not overcome, if you begin to sink, say, "Lord, I perish, save me." Say, "I perish," that you perish not. For He only can deliver you from the death of the body, who died in the body for you. Let us turn to the Lord.

Ephrem the Syrian (306-373)

Ephrem was born in Nisbis (modern day Syria) and raised in a pagan household, but was eventually baptized by Bishop James of Nisbis at the age of 18. Later Ephrem went to live in Edessa (modern day Iraq) where he was ordained a deacon. As a deacon he was given permission to preach and from later writers we know that he was considered a very good preacher. Ephrem was never ordained to the priesthood, but this did not prevent him from fulfilling his ministry in the Church. Ephrem was an avid writer and wrote numerous hymns on liturgical feasts in the Church year as well as full commentaries on books of scripture. This particular sermon or hymn on repentance reminds us of the simplicity of Jesus' command to "come and follow me." These hymns were used in a liturgical setting and therefore are quite different than a sermon or homily. Ephrem is commemorated together with Isaac the Syrian on January 28.

For Further Reading:

Ephrem the Syrian *Hymns on Paradise* translated by Sebastian Brock (Crestwood, NY: St. Vladimir's Seminary Press, 1990).

Ephrem the Syrian: *Hymns* translated by Kathleen McVey (Mahwah, NJ: Paulist Press, 1989).

Homily on Admonition and Repentance

1. Not of compulsion is the doctrine; of free-will is the word of life. Whoso is willing to hear the doctrine, let him cleanse the field of his will that the good seed fall not among the thorns of vain enquirings. If you would heed the word of life, cut yourself off from evil things; the hearing of the word profits nothing to the man that is busied with sins. If you will to be good, love not dissolute customs. First of all, trust in God, and then hearken to His law.

2. You can not hear His words, while you do not know yourself; and if you keep His judgments while your understanding is aloof from Him, who will give you your reward? Who will keep for you your recompense? You were baptised in His Name; confess His Name! In the Persons and in the naming, Father and Son and Holy Spirit, three Names and Persons, these three shall be a wall to you, against divisions and wranglings. Doubt not of the truth, lest you perish through the truth. You were baptised from the water; you have put on Christ in His naming; the seat of the Lord is on your person and His stamp on your forehead. See that you become not another's, for other Lord have you none. One is He Who formed us in His mercy; one is He Who redeemed us on His cross. He it is Who guides our life; He it is Who has power over our feebleness; He it is Who brings to pass our Resurrection. He rewards us according to our works. Blessed is he that confesses Him, and hears and keeps His commandments! You, O man, are a son of God Who is high over all. See that you vex not by your works the Father Who is good and gracious.

3. If you are angry against your neighbour, you are angry against God; and if you bear anger in your heart, against your Lord is your boldness uplifted. If in envy you rebuke, wicked is all your reproof. But if charity dwell in you, you have on earth no enemy. And if you are a true son of peace, you will stir up wrath in no man. If you are just and upright, you will not do wrong to your fellow. And if you love to be angry, be angry with the wicked and it will become you; if to wage war you seek, lo! Satan is your adversary; if you desire to revile, against the demons display your curses. If you should insult the King's image, you shall pay the penalty of murder; and if you revile a man, you revile the image of God. Do honour to your neighbour, and lo! you have honoured God. But if you would dishonour Him, in wrath assail your neighbour!

4. *This is the first Commandment,—You shall love the Lord your God with all your heart and your soul, and with your might* according as you are able. The sign that you love God, is this, that you love your fellow; and if you hate your fellow, your hatred is towards God. For it is blasphemy if you pray before God while you

are angry. For your heart also convicts you, that in vain you multiply words: your conscience rightly judges that in your prayers you profit nought. Christ as He hung on the height of the tree, interceded for His murderers; and you (who art) dust, son of the clay, rage fills you at its will. You keep anger against your brother; and do you yet dare to pray? Even he that stands on your side, though he be not neighbour to your sins, the taint of iniquity reaches unto him, and his petition is not heard. Leave off rage and then pray; and unless you would further provoke, restrain anger and so shall you supplicate. And if he (the other) is not to encounter you in fury, banish rage from that body, because it is holden with lusts.

5. You have a spiritual nature; the soul is the image of the Creator; honour the image of God, by being in agreement with all men. Remember death, and be not angry, that your peace be not of constraint. As long as your life remains to you, cleanse your soul from wrath; for if it should go to Sheol with you, your road will be straight to Gehenna. Keep not anger in your heart; hold not fury in your soul; you have not power over your soul, save to do that which is good. You are bought with the blood of God; you are redeemed by the passion of Christ; for your sake He suffered death, that you might die to your sins. His face endured spitting, that you might not shrink from scorn. Vinegar and gall did He drink, that you might be set apart from wrath. He received stripes on His body, that you might not fear suffering. If you are in truth His servant, fear your holy Lord; if you are His true disciple, walk in your Master's footsteps. Endure scorn from your brother, that you may be the companion of Christ. Display not anger against man, that you be not set apart from your Redeemer.

6. You are a man, the dust of the earth, clay, kinsman of the clod; you are the son of the race of beasts. If you know not your honour; separate your soul from animals, by works and not by words. If you love derision, you are altogether as Satan; and if you mock at your fellow, you are the mouth of the Devil; if against defects and flaws, in (injurious) names you delight, Satan is not in creation but his place you have seized by force. Get you far, O man, from this; for it is altogether hurtful; and if you desire to live well, sit not with the scorner, lest you become the partner of his sin and of his punishment. Hate mockery which is altogether (the cause of weeping), and mirth which is (the cause of) cleansing. And if you should hear a mocker by chance, when you are not desiring it, sign yourself with the cross of light, and hasten from thence like an antelope. Where Satan lodges, Christ will in nowise dwell; a spacious dwelling for Satan is the man that mocks at his neighbour; a palace of the Enemy is the heart of the mocker. Satan does not desire to add any other evil to it. Mockery is sufficient for him to supply the place of all. Neither his belly nor yet his purse can (the sinner) fill with that

sin of his. By his laughter is the wretch despoiled, and he knows not nor does he perceive it. For his wound, there is no cure; for his sickness, there is no healing; his pain, admits no remedy; and his sore, endures no medicine. I desire not with such a one to put forth my tongue to reprove him: enough for him is his own shame; sufficient for him is his boldness. Blessed is he that has not heard him; and blessed is he that has not known him. Be it far from you, O Church, that he should enter you, that evil leaven of Satan!

7. Narrow is the way of life, and broad the way of torment; prayer is able to bring a man to the house of the kingdom. This is the perfect work; prayer that is pure from iniquity. The righteousness of man is as nothing accounted. The work of men, what is it? His labour is altogether vanity. Of You, O Lord, of Your grace it is that in our nature we should become good. Of You is righteousness, that we from men should become righteous. Of You is the mercy and favour, that we from the dust should become Your image. Give power to our will, that we be not sunk in sin! Pour into our heart memory, that at every hour we may know Your honour! Plant truth in our minds, that we perish not among doubts! Occupy our understanding with Your law, that it wander not in vain thoughts! Order the motions of our members, that they bring no hurt upon us! Draw near to God, that Satan may flee from you. Cast out passions from your heart, and lo! you have put to flight the enemy. Hate sins and wickedness, and Satan at once will have fled. Whatsoever sins you serve, you are worshipping secret idols. Whatsoever transgressions you love, you are serving demons in your soul. Whensoever you strive with your brother, Satan abides in peace. Whensoever you envy your fellow, you give rest to Devils. Whensoever you tell the shortcoming of others who are not present, your tongue has made a harp for the music of the devil. Whensoever hatred is in your soul, great is the peace of the Deceiver. Whensoever you love incantations, your labour is altogether of the left hand. If you love unseemly discourse, you prepare a feast for demons. For this is the worship of idols, the working of the lusts (of the flesh).

8. If so be you give a gift in pride, this is not of God. If you are lifted up by reason of your knowledge, you have denied the grace of God. If you are poor and proud, lo! your end is in your torment. If you are haughty and needy, lo! your need is toward your destruction. If you are sick and criest out, lo! your trouble is full of harm. If you are in need of food, yet your mind longs for riches; your distress is with the poor, but your torment with the rich. If you shall look unchastely, and shall desire your neighbour's wife, lo! your portion shall be with the adulterers, and your hell with the fornicators. *Let your own fountain be for yourself, and drink waters from your well. Let your fountains be for yourself alone,*

and let not another drink with you. Require purity of your body as you require of your yoke-fellow. You would not have her commit lewdness, the wife of your youth, with another man; commit not lewdness with another woman, the wife of a different husband. Let the defilement of her be hateful in your eyes; keep aloof from it altogether. Chastity beseems the wife; purity is as her adornment; law becomes the husband; justice is the crown for his head. Desire not the bed of your neighbour lest another desire your bed. Preserve purity in your marriage, that your marriage may be holy. His conscience reproves the man, who corrupts the wife of his neighbour. He fears, and deceives through terror, whoso has engaged in fornication. Darkness is dearer to him than light, whose manner of life is not pure. Every hour he stands in dread, who commits adultery secretly. The adulterer is also a thief who breaks into houses in darkness. The very place reproves him, where he does the evil and wickedness. He enters the chamber and sins; in the darkness he does his will. The time will come when it shall be disclosed, when his secret deeds shall be manifested. With what eyes do you look towards God in prayer? What hands do you raise when you ask pardon? Be ashamed and dismayed for yourself, that you are void of understanding. If when your neighbour see you, you are ashamed and dismayed, how much more should you be ashamed before God Who sees all? You are like the sow, your companion, that wallows altogether in mire. Even in seeing, you may sin, if your mind is not watchful; and in hearing you may transgress, if you do not guard your hearing. The fornicator's heart waxes wanton through speech that is full of uncleanness. The passion hidden in the mind, sight and hearing awaken it.

9. He puts on garments of shame who desires to commit fornication, that from the lust of raiment, lewdness may enter and dwell in his heart. Make not snares of your garments for that which is openly wanton. Speak not a word in craftiness, nor dig your neighbour's well. Look not after the harlot; be not snared by the beauty of her face. She is even as the dog that is mad, yea, much more bold than it. Modesty is removed from her face, she knows not what shame is. With spitting accept her person; with reviling meet herself; with a rod pursue her like a dog, for she is like one, and to be compared with such. Reject the sweetness of her words lest you fall into her net. She empties purses and wallets, and her gains are without number. Flee from her, for she is the daughter of vipers, that she tear not in pieces your whole body.

10. You shall not slander any man, lest they call you Satan. If you hate the name, go not near to the act; but if you love the act, be not angry at the name. Count yourself rebuked first of all by the beasts and birds, how that every kind cleaves to its kind; and so agree with your yokefellow. Rejoice not in men's dish-

onour, that you become not a Satan yourself. If evil should happen to him that hates you, see that you rejoice not, lest you sin. If your adversary should fall, be in pain and mourning. Keep your heart with all diligence, that it sin not in secret; for there is to be a laying bare of thoughts and of actions. Employ your hands in labour, and let your heart meditate in prayer. Love not vain discourse, for discourse that shall be profitable alike to the soul and the body lightens the burden of your labour.

11. Does the poor man cry at your door? Arise and open for him gladly: refresh him when he is wearied; sustain his heart, for it is sad. You know by experience the affliction of poverty: receive not others in your house, and drive not out the beggar. Have you also a law, a comely law for your household. Establish an order that is wise, that the abjects laugh not at you. Be careful in all your doings, that you be not a sport for fools; be upright and prudent, and both simple and wise. Let your body be quiet and cheerful, your greeting seemly and simple; your discourse without fault, your speech brief and savoury; your words few and sound, full of savour and understanding. Speak not overmuch, not even words that are wise; for all things that are over many, though they be wise are wearisome.—To them of your household be as a father. Amongst your brethren esteem yourself least, and inferior amongst your fellows, and of little account with all men. With your friend keep a secret; to those that love you be true. See that there be no wrangling; the secrets of your friends reveal not, lest all that hear you hate you and esteem you a mischiefmaker. With those that hate you wrangle not, neither face to face nor yet in your heart. No enemy shall you have but Satan his very self. Give counsel to the wife you have wedded; give heed to her doings; as stronger you are answerable that you should sustain her weakness. For weak is womankind, and very ready to fall. Be as a hawk, when kindled (to anger), but when wrath departs from you, be gladsome and also firm, in the blending of diverse qualities. Keep silence among the aged; to the elders give due honour. Honour the priests with diligence, as good stewards of the household. Give due honour to their degree, and search not out their doings. In his degree the priest is an angel, but in his doings a man. By mercy he is made a mediator, between God and mankind.

12. Search not out the faults of men; reveal not the sin of your fellow; the shortcomings of your neighbours, in speech of the mouth repeat not. You are not judge in creation, you have not dominion over the earth. If you love righteousness, reprove your soul and yourself. Be judge unto your own sins, and chastener of your own transgressions. Make not inquiry maliciously, into the misdeeds of men. For if you do this, injuries will not be lacking to you. Trust not the hearing

of the ear, for many are the deceivers. Vain reports believe not, for false rumours are not few.

13. Regard not spells and divinations, for that is communion with Satan. Love not idle prating, not even in behalf of righteousness. Discourse concerning yourself begin not, even in behalf of what is becoming. Flee and hide yourself from wrangling, as from a violent robber. See that you be not a surety in a loan, lest you sin. According as you have, assist him, (even) the man that is poorer than you. Mock not the foolish man; pray that you be not even as he. Him that sins blame not, lest you also be put to confusion. To him that repents of his sins be a helper and counsellor, and encourage him that is able to rise. Let him hold fast hope in God, and his sin shall be burned as stubble. Visit the sick and be not wearied, that you may be beloved of men. Be familiar with the house of mourning, but a stranger to the house of feasting. Be not constant in drinking wine, lest your shortcomings multiply. Cast a wall round your lips, and set a guard upon your mouth; endure suffering with your neighbour and share also in his tribulation. A good friend in tribulation is made known to him that loves him. In charity follow the deceased, with sorrow and with offerings, and pray that he may have rest in the hidden place whither he is going.

14. When you stand in prayer, cry in your soul: Have mercy on me, I am a sinner and weak; be gracious, O God, to my weakness, and grant strength to me to pray a prayer that shall be pleasing to Your Will. "Punish not mine enemies, take not vengeance on them that hate me; but grant them in Your grace that they may become doers of Your Will." At the time of prayer and petition, continue in contemplations such as these continue. Bow your head before the Mighty One.

15. Do not resist evil, for he is evil from the Evil One, whoso resists evil. Keep not back anything from any man, that if he perishes you may not be blamed. Change not your respect for a man's person, according to goods and possessions. Make all things as though they were not and God alone were in being. If you shall ask of your neighbour and he shall not give you according to your wish, see that you say not in anger a word that is full of bitterness. Oppose not [fit] seasons, for many are the changes. Put sorrow far from your flesh, and sadness from your thoughts; save only that for your sins you should be constant in sadness. Cease not from labour, not even though you be rich, for the slothful man gains manifold guilt by his idleness.

16. Be a lover of poverty, and be desirous of neediness. If you have them both for your portion, you are an inheritor on high. Despise not the voice of the poor and give him not cause to curse you. For if he curse whose palate is bitter, the Lord will hear his petition. If his garments are foul, wash them in water, which

freely is bought. Has a poor man entered into your house? God has entered into your house; God dwells within your abode. He, whom you have refreshed from his troubles, from troubles will deliver you. Have you washed the feet of the stranger? You have washed away the filth of your sins. Have you prepared a table before him? Behold God eating [at it], and Christ likewise drinking [at it], and the Holy Spirit resting [on it]: Is the poor satisfied at your table and refreshed? You have satisfied Christ your Lord. He is ready to be your rewarder; in presence of angels and men He will confess you have fed His hunger; He will give thanks unto you that you gave Him drink, and quenched His thirst.

17. O how gracious is the Lord! O how measureless are His mercies! Happy the race of mortals when God confesses it! Woe to the soul which He denies! Fire is stored up for its punishment. Be of good cheer, my son, in hope; sow good [seed] and faint not. The husbandman sows in hope, and the merchant journeys in hope, you also love good [seed]; in the hope look for the reward. Do nothing at all without the beginning of prayer. With the sign of the living cross, seal all your doings, my son. Go not forth from the door of your house till you have signed the cross. Whether in eating or in drinking, whether in sleeping or in waking, whether in your house or on the road, or again in the season of leisure, neglect not this sign; for there is no guardian like it. It shall be unto you as a wall, in the forefront of all your doings. And teach this to your children, that heedfully they be conformed to it.

18. Yoke yourself under the law, that you may be a freeman in very truth. Work not the desire of your soul apart from the law of God. How many commandments must I write, and how many laws must I engrave; which, if you desire your freedom, you can learn all from yourself? And if you love purity, you will teach it to others also. Let nature be your book, and all creation your tables; and learn from them the laws, and meditate things unwritten. The sun in his course teaches you that you rest from labour. The night in her silence cries to you that a limit is set to your works. The earth and the fruit of the tree cry that there is a season for all things. The seed you sow in the winter, in the summer you gather its harvest. Thus in the world sow seeds of righteousness, and in the Resurrection gather them in. The bird in its daily gleaning reproves the covetous and his greed, and rebukes the extortion that grasps the store of others. Death, the limit of all things, is itself the reprover of all things.

19. Take refuge in God Who passes not away nor is changed. Restrain laughter by suffering, and mirthfulness by sorrow. Console suffering by hope, and sadness by expectation. Believe and trust, you that art wise, for God is He Who guides you; and if His care leaves you not, there is nothing that can harm you. If

one man by another man, the lowly by the great, can be saved, how much more shall the refuge of God preserve the man that believes? Fear not because of adversaries who with violence come upon you. He will watchfully guard your soul, and hurtful things become profitable. No one shall lead you by compulsion, save only where there is freedom. No one falls into temptation, that passes the measure of his strength. There is no evil in chastisement, if so be that freedom is willing. The doings are not perverse of freedom, its will is perverted.

20. To men that are just and upright, temptations become helps. Job, a man of discernment, was victorious in temptations. Sickness came upon him, and he complained not; disease afflicted him and he murmured not; his body failed and his strength departed, but his will was not weakened. He proved perfect in all by sufferings, for as much as temptations crushed him not. Abraham was a stranger, from his place, his race [and his kindred]. But by this he was not harmed; nay rather he triumphed greatly. So Joseph from the house of bondage was made to rule as king of Egypt. They of the company of Ananias and Daniel delivered others from bondage. See then, O you that are wise, the power that freedom possesses; that nothing can injure it unless the will is weakened. Israel with sumptuous living waxed fat, and kicked, and forgot his covenant. He worshipped vain gods, and forgot the nature of his creation. The bondage that was in Egypt he forgat in the repose of the desert. As often as he was afflicted, he acknowledged the Lord alone; but when he was dwelling in repose, he forgot God his Redeemer. Seek not here repose, for this is a world of toil. And if you can wisely discern, change not time for time; that which abides for that which abides not; that which ceases not for that which ceases; nor truth for lying; nor body for shadow; nor watching for slumber; nor that which is in season for that which is out of season; nor the Time for the times. Collect your mind, let it not wander among varieties which profit not.

21. No one in creation is rich but he that fears God; no one is truly poor but he that lacks the truth. How needy is he, and not rich, whose need witnesses against him that even from the abject and the beggars he needs to receive a gift. He is truly a bondman, and many are his masters: he renders service to money, to riches, and possessions. His lords are void of mercy, for they grant him no repose. Flee, and live in poverty; (as) a mother she pities her beloved. Seek refuge in indigence, who nourishes her children with choice things; her yoke is light and pleasant, and sweet to the palate her memory. The sick in conscience alone abhors the draught of poverty; the fainthearted dreads the yoke of indigence that is honourable. Who has granted to You, Son of man, in the world to find repose? Who has granted to you, thing of dust, to be rich amidst poverty? Be not through

desires needy and looking to others. Sufficient for you is your daily bread, that comes of the sweat of your face. Let this be (the measure of your need, that which the day gives you; and if you find for yourself a feast, take of it that which you need. You shall not take in a day (the provision) of days, for the belly keeps no treasure. Praise and give thanks when you are satisfied, that therein you provoke not the Giver to anger. In purity strengthen yourself, that you may gain from it profit. In everything give thanks and praise unto God as the Redeemer, that He may grant you by His grace, that we may hear and do His Will.

You to whom I have given the counsel of life, be not negligent in it. From that which is other men's (doctrine) have I written to you; see that you despise not their words. And if I depart before you, in your prayer make mention of me. In every season pray and beseech that our love may continue true. But as for us, on behalf of these things let us offer up praise and honour to Father, to Son, and to Holy Spirit, now and for ever. Amen.

Bibliography

General References For Scripture Study:

Bianchi, Enzo. *Praying the Word: An Introduction to Lectio Divina*. Kalamazoo, MI: Cistercian Publications, 1998.

Johnson, Luke Timothy. *Living Jesus: Learning the Heart of the Gospel*. San Fransisco, CA: Harper Collins, 1999.

Manley, Johanna. *The Bible and the Holy Fathers*. Crestwood, NY: St. Vladimir's Seminary Press.

Mills, William C. *From Pascha to Pentecost: Reflections on the Gospel of John*. Rollinsford, NH: Orthodox Research Institute, 2004.

--------------------*Prepare O Bethlehem: Reflections on the Gospel Readings for Nativity and Epiphany*. Rolllinsford, NH: Orthodox Research Institute, 2005.

--------------------*Baptize All Nations: Reflections on the Gospel of Matthew During the Pentecost Season*. Rollinsford, NH: Orthodox Research Institute, 2006.

-------------------- *A Light to the Gentiles: Reflections on the Gospel of Luke*. NY, iUniverse, 2007.

Royster, Archbishop Dmitri. *The Parables*. Crestwood, NY: St. Vladimir's Seminary Press, 1996.

-------------------- *The Miracles of Christ*. Crestwood, NY: St Vladimir's Seminary Press, 1999.

-------------------- *The Epistle to the Hebrews*. Crestwood, NY: St. Vladimir's Seminary Press, 2003.

-------------------- *The Epistle to the Romans*. Crestwood, NY: St. Vladimir's Seminary Press, forthcoming 2007.

Internet Resources for Scripture Study:

Orthodox Center for the Advancement of Biblical Studies www.ocabs.org

New Testament Gateway www.ntgateway.com

PBS Documentary "From Jesus To Christ" www.pbs.org/wbgh/page/frontline/show/religion

Select Commentaries on the Gospel of Mark:

Tarazi, Paul N. *The New Testament Introduction: Paul and Mark.* Crestwood, NY: St. Vladimir's Seminary Press, 1999.

About the Author

Fr. William Mills, Ph.D. is the rector of the Nativity of the Holy Virgin Orthodox Church in Charlotte, NC, as well as an adjunct professor of religious studies at Queens University in Charlotte, NC. Fr. Mills received his Bachelor of History from Millersville University of Pennsylvania and then pursued theological studies at Saint Vladimir's Theological Orthodox Seminary in Crestwood, NY where he received both a Master of Divinity and Master of Theology degrees. He then pursued advanced theological studies at the Union Institute and University in Cincinnati, Ohio where he received his doctorate in Pastoral Theology. Fr. Mills is also the author of *From Pascha to Pentecost: Reflections on the Gospel of John* (Rollinsford, NH: Orthodox Research Institute, 2005), *Prepare O Bethlehem: Reflections on the Scripture Readings for Christmas-Epiphany* (Rollinsford, NH: Orthodox Research Institute, 2006), and *Baptize All Nations: Reflections on the Gospel of Matthew* (Rollinsford, NH: Orthodox Research Institute, 2007). Fr. Mills is available for parish and clergy retreats. Visit his personal website at www.wcmills.com.

978-0-595-48044-9
0-595-48044-6

Printed in the United States
100320LV00004B/295-333/A

9 780595 480449